Parties for Children

*Ideas and Instructions for Invitations,
Decorations, Refreshments, Favors,
Crafts and Games for 19 Theme Parties*

DEBRA K. MOORE *and*
JACQUELINE A. KUTTER

Illustrations by Marita Wassman

McFarland & Company, Inc., Publishers
Jefferson, North Carolina, and London

The present work is a reprint of the library bound edition of
Parties for Children: Ideas and Instructions for Invitations,
Decorations, Refreshments, Favors, Crafts and Games for 19
Theme Parties, *first published in 1995 by McFarland.*

LIBRARY OF CONGRESS CATALOGUING-IN-PUBLICATION DATA

Moore, Debra K., 1958–
    Parties for children : ideas and instructions for invitations,
decorations, refreshments, favors, crafts and games for 19 theme
parties / Debra K. Moore and Jacqueline A. Kutter ;
illustrations by Marita Wassman.
        p.   cm.
    Includes bibliographical references and index.

    ISBN 978-0-7864-7283-3
    softcover : acid free paper ∞

    1. Children's parties.   I. Kutter, Jacqueline A.   II. Title.
GV1205.M66 2012
793.2'1—dc20   95-2594

BRITISH LIBRARY CATALOGUING DATA ARE AVAILABLE

Cover art © 2012 Hemera/Thinkstock

Manufactured in the United States of America

McFarland & Company, Inc., Publishers
    Box 611, Jefferson, North Carolina 28640
        www.mcfarlandpub.com

Thanks to Amy and Eric who gave me the
experience necessary to be a party planning
expert and to Michael whose encouragement
and support never waivered. — Debra

Dedicated to my children Julie and David,
for without them I would not have seen the
need for this book. They were my inspiration
and my experimenters. Special thanks to my
husband Ray for his loving patience and
encouragement. — Jackie

Contents

Introduction

When you choose to plan a party for children, you are giving them a very special gift. Because we love children, we want to make them happy on their special day. What better way to express our love than with a wonderful celebration.

Understanding the child's expectations is the key to a successful party. Children do not consider the cost or the time it takes for preparation. This book was written to help you produce a party that fulfills a child's desires, while keeping the amount of work and the cost to a minimum. For each of the party themes, we have given directions for invitations, decorations, refreshments, party favors, crafts and games. Choose ideas that fit the needs, ages, and abilities of the children.

The information in this book will satisfy all your planning needs and make the party an enjoyable one for both adult and child. Remember, the best thing about a party is friends gathered together for a celebration.

PLANNING

Designing a party which matches a child's wishes is easier than you may think. A child's idea of fun is to give a party with lots of friends, decorations, games, and good things to eat. Involve the child in the planning process. Even young children have definite ideas about themes, treats, and games for parties. Let the child help as much as possible. By nature, children are "doers" not observers, and they will take pride in a party they have helped to plan.

Organization and planning are essential ingredients for a party's success. Start planning at least four weeks in advance. Use a checklist for everything (see pages 7–9). Refer to it often. No detail is insignificant. A complete party plan leads to a successful party.

Outline your party schedule in sequence. Knowing the exact order of the series of events will assure a smooth flow to the celebration. There should be a definite beginning, middle, and end to the party. Plan a full agenda. Do not leave any periods of unplanned time. Most games and activities take less time than you may think so plan accordingly. Prepare backup activities.

A successful party begins with activities that go along with the children's excitement and energy level. Divide a large party into groups that rotate through the activities. Plan a final activity that brings all the children together and indicates an end to the party. On your party schedule, write the planned time of each game and a brief reminder of the rules. List the specific starting and ending times of each activity. Try to keep yourself on schedule and know where you can be flexible, if necessary. A party schedule might be similar to the following example:

1:30–1:40	activity as guests are arriving
1:40–1:50	game
1:50–2:00	game
2:00–2:15	craft time
2:15–2:30	open gifts
2:30–2:45	serve refreshments
2:45–2:55	final group activity
2:55–3:00	distribute party favors

THEME

To begin planning, decide on a party theme. A central idea will make the party more exciting and easier to plan. It provides the focus for the day's events.

The theme should reflect the interests and age of the child. Personalizing the theme to the child's interest will make the party special. Ideas in this book can be adapted to your own party theme. A favorite animal, popular movie, or special activity in which the child is involved can be the base for building a fun-filled party. Themes can be seasonal or deliberately out of season, such as Christmas in July or baseball in January.

The theme should be carried throughout the party. Invitations, decorations, crafts, games, refreshments, and favors should all reflect the party theme.

INVITATIONS

You do not have to be an artist in order to design your own party invitations. A simple picture colored by a child can make a cute invitation. Incorporate the theme into the invitation. Construction paper, blank postcards, stickers, and stencils create unique invitations.

Invitations should include all of the following information: name of the child hosting the party, location and directions to the party, date of the party, starting and ending time of the party, the RSVP phone number, and the date you are requesting a reply.

If the party requires the guest to bring special items (doll, paint smock, sleeping bag, etc.), include this information on the invitation. Be sure to note if special clothing (bathing suit, dress-up, mix-up, etc.) is required.

Keep the party small and controllable. Additional children do not necessarily mean additional party fun. Large groups can overstimulate a party situation. Attention from too many people can be overwhelming to a young child. Keep the ages of the guests invited to the party to within a year or two of each other. Rule of thumb — the younger the person, the fewer the guests. The following is a suggested guideline:

3–4 year olds: 6–8 guests
5–7 year olds: 8–10 guests
8–10 year olds: 12–15 guests

Send the invitations to the guests at least two weeks prior to the party. Do not pass them out at school unless everyone of the same gender in the class is invited. It will be impossible to keep the party a secret, and someone who did not receive an invitation will feel left out.

DECORATIONS

Decorating the party area creates a festive atmosphere. It transforms an ordinary setting into the location of a very special occasion. It can also define the space perimeters you wish to establish. Allow plenty of space, but confine the party to one specific area.

Design decorations to fit the theme of the party. Posters, calendar pictures, paper dolls, and coloring book pictures make great decorations. Balloons, crepe paper streamers, and construction paper are inexpensive items that can change a plain room into a festive one. Each chapter in this book will give you a choice of decorating ideas you can make with materials usually found in the home.

Decide before the party if you will keep the decorations or send them home with the guests as party favors. If you are giving them to the guests, be sure there will be enough for everyone (including the child hosting the party) and that everyone will receive similar or identical items.

REFRESHMENTS

Refreshments should be geared toward the theme of the party. Each party plan in this book offers a variety of snack, meal, and treat ideas relating to that party theme. Choose a simple cake design or serve a healthy meal accented with sweet treats.

When planning refreshments, serve foods children like to eat. Keep it simple. Children are rarely impressed with a trendy, gourmet recipe. Certain foods are necessary for a healthy diet, but can be very uninteresting at special party celebrations.

Be ready. Prepare all food in advance. If possible, arrange serving-sized portions prior to the party. Enlist a volunteer to help with any food that must be prepared during the party, so you can be involved in the party activities and prevent any "down" time for the children.

If serving a meal, plan for additional time at the party. Prepare enough food to have plenty of extras. It is a myth that children are always too excited to eat at parties. It is better to have leftovers than not to have enough.

Do not allow the children to leave the refreshment table until everyone is finished eating. This maintains control, prevents the children from wandering off unsupervised, and makes it easier to move to the next group activity.

PARTY FAVORS

Distributing party favors will give your party a happy ending. Favors are a way of saying to each guest, "Thank you for coming to my party."

Coordinate the party favors with the theme. Fill a decorated paper bag with inexpensive treats and you have made a party favor or goody bag. Label the favors with each guest's name and keep them by the exit to hand out as the guests leave. The goodies are guaranteed to be used and misplaced if received before the party is over. If the favors are passed out during the party, keep extra favors on hand to replace items which have been lost, broken or eaten by another child. Also, prepare a party favor for the birthday child. If not, the child is sure to prefer it over any of the gifts received.

CRAFTS

Craft projects offer an opportunity for everyone to participate in something at the same time. They are noncompetitive and can be geared toward the children's level of development. Plan on making one craft during the party. Keep crafts simple. Children enjoy making something they can wear or use. Crafts encourage the children to be creative and give everyone a sense of accomplishment.

Choose crafts to fit the theme of your party. This book offers a selection of craft ideas appropriate for various age levels. The craft ideas can be adapted from one theme to another.

Be prepared. Make a model of the craft for the children. Gather all the materials together and place them in a convenient location. Keep extra materials on hand to allow for error.

GAMES

A fun party includes three to five games which fit the party theme. The games in this book can be adapted from one party to another. Keep in mind the ages of the guests when planning activities. If something is too easy, the children will not like it. If the activity is too hard, they will become frustrated. If a game involves reading, be sure all of the children can read. If the party has a wide range of ages, the younger guests can be busy with a simple activity, such as coloring or batting a balloon attached to the ceiling, while the older children are playing other games.

The best games, particularly for younger children, require cooperation rather than individual competition. Team relays or games without one specific winner are fun and encourage the spirit of cooperation. It is best if a game does not end with one child being eliminated from the game. If so, immediately involve the child that gets eliminated in another activity.

Clap and cheer for every player. Children understand winning but can have a difficult time with losing. Refrain from awarding prizes for each activity to avoid conflicts. Every child enjoys being acknowledged for giving his best effort.

If you choose to give prizes to the winners, have consolation prizes for the other participants, such as candy or stickers. Keep plenty of prizes on hand. Extras will be necessary in case of ties or to resolve conflicts.

Prior to the party, gather all the materials together and place them in a convenient location. Plan an activity that can be played as guests are arriving. Without this activity, the children will become restless and get tired of waiting. Boredom will lead them into creating their own activities. Before their behavior gets out-of-control, involve them in the party festivities.

GIFTS

At a well-organized party, all of the children will be busy during the opening of the presents. Play a game of chance and, as each guest "wins," she will then give her gift. Or, all the children can sit in a circle passing around each gift.

As the guests arrive at the party, place the gifts in a remote location until you are ready to open them. Remind the birthday child to open one gift at a time, to read the card, and to thank the giver. Also, remind him before the party of what to say if he receives a duplicate gift or a gift he dislikes.

Do not allow the guests to open any toys or play with the presents. The birthday child should be the first to enjoy each new item after the party is over. When the gifts are played with at the party, there is the risk of items being broken or pieces being misplaced.

Be prepared to have someone write down what gift came from which guest. Send thank-you notes. A young child can draw a thank-you picture, and an older child can sign his name or write a brief message.

HELPFUL HINTS

Show some extra compassion for the child during the busy party preparation time. Birthdays and holidays are exciting, but the anticipation is often too stressful for children. Planning activities to keep the child busy beforehand can help him to relax. Avoid giving him excessive sweets and caffeine. Make countdown rings or a countdown calendar to help the child visualize the waiting period.

Allow for the different personalities of the children. Some may be shy or not wish to participate in a planned activity. If not forced to play, the child will probably join in at some point. It is important, however, that all the children be supervised and not allowed to wander off.

Understand your own limitations. Enlist family and friends to help during the party. We recommend one adult for every six children. Older siblings can be valuable party helpers. Volunteers appreciate knowing what to do and when it is to be done. Give each child a name tag to assist the party volunteers.

Plan for a volunteer to assist with taking pictures. Pictures capture special memories and you will be too busy to snap those photos yourself. If possible, videotape the celebration to enjoy later.

Take time to recap the party. After the guests have left, spend a few moments with the child remembering the event. Find out which game was his favorite and which gift he liked best. Remind him of a funny incident. Review the photos and video and you can, again, enjoy the fun.

Preparation Checklist

Date Completed	Things to Do
_____	Decide party theme
_____	Plan guest list

	Guest	RSVP
1	_____	☐
2	_____	☐
3	_____	☐
4	_____	☐
5	_____	☐
6	_____	☐
7	_____	☐
8	_____	☐
9	_____	☐
10	_____	☐
11	_____	☐
12	_____	☐
13	_____	☐
14	_____	☐
15	_____	☐

_____	Make invitations
_____	Mail invitations

Date Completed	Things to Do
_____	Make decorations
_____	Make party favors
_____	Make sample craft
_____	Prepare games
	1 _____
	2 _____
	3 _____
	4 _____
_____	Enlist volunteers
	1 _____
	2 _____
	3 _____
_____	Prepare refreshments

Shopping List

Things to Make	Supplies Needed
Invitations	_____
	_____
	_____
Decorations	_____
	_____
	_____
Refreshments and paper products	_____
	_____
	_____
Party favors	_____
	_____
	_____
Crafts	_____
	_____
	_____
Games	_____
	_____
	_____

Animal Party

INVITATIONS

• Fold a piece of brown construction paper and cut a monkey shape on the fold line (see below). On the outside of the invitation write, "For a swinging time, come monkey around at my party!" Write the necessary party information on the inside of the invitation.

• Cut a large animal shape from a piece of heavy paper or poster board. Write the invitation information on the animal and cut the invitation into five or six puzzle pieces. Place these pieces into an envelope and deliver to the guests.

DECORATIONS

1. Place paw prints on the ground leading to the party area.
2. Attach a large cutout of an animal to the entrance door.
3. Draw the face of an animal and attach it to the front of your mailbox. Make a tail for the rear of the mailbox.
4. Decorate the party area with plush animals.
5. Make animal shapes from inflated balloons or draw animal faces onto balloons.
6. Create a zoo. The animal cages can be made from large cardboard boxes. To make bars, cut out 1-inch strips around the sides of the boxes. Place plush animals inside the cages peeking out.

REFRESHMENTS

Teddy Bear Cake: Bake your favorite cake mix in a 9″×13″ pan. After the cake has cooled, cut out one circle 7 inches in diameter and one 4½-inch circle. Cut out four small ovals for the feet and arms and two small circles for the ears (see below). Position the pieces on a prepared cake board and connect with chocolate frosting. With a toothpick, draw a mouth in the head and an oval in the stomach. Frost the mouth and

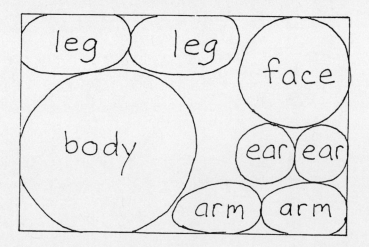

stomach with white frosting. Frost the rest of the bear with chocolate frosting and decorate with chocolate sprinkles. Decorate the face with assorted candies and licorice (see above).

Birds' Nests:

3 cups crispy rice cereal	¾ cup peanut butter
⅓ cup light corn syrup	1 teaspoon vanilla
½ cup brown sugar	36 jelly beans

Bring the corn syrup, brown sugar, peanut butter and vanilla to a boil. Remove from heat. Stir in the cereal. Let cool until touchable. Shape into balls the size of a medium orange and put into muffin pans. Push down in the middle, pressing towards the sides of the muffin pan. Indent the middle of the nest with your thumb. Add three jelly beans to represent the bird eggs. Makes twelve nests.

Elephant Eater Food Bar: Children with big (elephant) appetites enjoy creating theirir own snack from this suggested food bar.
- Offer a choice of a taco shell or a soft, flour tortilla and an assortment of fillings, such as meat, shredded cheese, diced tomatoes, shredded lettuce, sour cream, chopped onion, or sliced olives.
- Make a fruit salad or have a selection of sliced apples, oranges, and grapes.
- Top crackers with peanut butter or cheese.
- Cut fruit flavored gelatin into bite-sized squares or animal shapes with a cookie cutter.

Big Bear Sundae: For each sundae put one scoop of chocolate ice cream into a bowl. Insert two round cookies for the ears and use small candies to make the eyes and nose.

PARTY FAVORS

• **Animal Nut Cups** can be made by the children or they can be made ahead of time to decorate the refreshment table. Fill the nut cups with treats, such as animal crackers, gummy bears, or peanuts (see below).

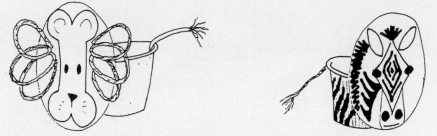

Suggestions: LION: Glue yarn loops around a 3-inch circle cut from poster board and draw a face on it. Glue the face onto the nut cup. For a tail, glue a piece of yarn to the rear of the cup and fray the end of the tail. ZEBRA: Cut a 3-inch circle from white poster board. Draw a face and black stripes on the circle, and glue onto the nut cup. Draw black stripes on the nut cup or glue black yarn up and down the nut cup to make the stripes. Glue a piece of yarn onto the back of the cup for a tail. POLAR BEAR: Glue cotton balls around the nut cup. Cut a 3-inch circle from white poster board. Draw a bear face on the circle and glue it to the cup. Cut two paws and a tail from the poster board and glue to the cup.

• A belly bag will make a great **Kangaroo Pouch** (see **For Kangaroos Only!** game on page 17). Fill with plastic animal toys, stickers, animal-shaped crayons, or animal sponges.

CRAFTS

Animal Magnets: From your local craft store, purchase flat wooden cutouts in animal shapes. Decorate with paints, markers, glue-on eyes, pom-pom tails, etc.

Cut a magnetic strip and glue it onto the back of the cutout, or thread the cutout with a small keychain.

Masks: Paper plates can be made into animal faces. Let the "party animals" decorate their masks with markers, crayons, sequins, pipe cleaners, yarn and pom-poms (see below). Attach a 12-inch piece of elastic to each side of the mask so the children can wear the faces.

Homemade Fundough:

1 cup flour	1 teaspoon powdered alum
½ cup salt	(or eliminate alum and use
1 cup water	1 tablespoon cream of tartar)
1 tablespoon cooking oil	5 to 7 drops food coloring
1 teaspoon cream of tartar	

Color the water with the food coloring. Mix all of the ingredients together. Heat, stirring constantly, until thick and rubbery. Remove from heat and wrap in waxed paper.

To keep the fundough moist, store it in an airtight plastic bag. The children can mold and shape the dough into their favorite animals. The animals can then be left out in the air to harden or stored in the plastic bags to be reused at home.

GAMES

Who's the Lion? All the guests will sit in a circle. Choose one player to be the wolf and have him leave the room. Choose one player to be the lion. The lion is the leader. The rest of the children are the lion cubs. Have the lion start doing a motion, such as clapping his hands, slapping his legs, patting his head, etc. and the cubs will mimic him. Send the wolf back into the room, and he will try to guess the identity of the lion. Meanwhile the lion is continuing to change motions and the cubs are following him, while trying not to be obvious that they are watching him. Give the wolf two guesses and then reveal the identity of the lion.

The lion then becomes the wolf. Appoint a new child to become the lion. The game continues until everyone has had a chance to be the wolf and the lion.

See the Monkey! Make a large monkey poster or paint a monkey on a board. This monkey needs to be tall enough to hide a child. Cut a hole large enough for a child's face to show through. When the guests arrive, take a picture of them as they put their face through the hole and become the monkey. You can give the guests their pictures when they are ready to leave or mail their pictures to them when you send the thank-you notes.

Monkey Business: Challenge the children to toss beanbags into the hole in the monkey poster (refer to **See the Monkey!** game above), moving them farther back with each successful toss.

Variation: Substitute wet sponges and toss at volunteers who put their faces in the monkey hole.

Animal Moves: Divide the children into teams and have each team stand in a line. Assign each child to be an animal during the relay. *Example:* The first child in each line is a monkey. He will need to walk like a monkey and make monkey sounds. The second child on each team will move and sound like a seal. The third child on each team is a frog and will be jumping and saying "Ribbitt, Ribbitt," etc.

Give the children a few minutes to practice each animal walk. They will enjoy moving and sounding like different animals and will understand what to do during the relay.

When the relay begins, the "animals" must go across the party area, around a stationary object and back to their line. As they cross their line, the next "animal" will begin. The first team to have all their animals complete the race is the winner.

Mr. Bear: Choose one person to be Mr. Bear. Mr. Bear is trying to sleep in his den which is approximately twenty feet from base. The other children will sneak up close to the sleeping bear and whisper, "Mr. Bear, are you awake?" Mr. Bear pretends not to hear them. The children then yell "MR. BEAR, ARE YOU AWAKE?" The growling bear jumps up and chases everyone, trying to catch as many as he can before they reach the base. Everyone tagged by Mr. Bear, before reaching base, becomes a bear cub and will help Mr. Bear catch the others on the next turn. The last person caught can begin as Mr. Bear when they play again.

For Kangaroos Only! For each guest, purchase a belly bag to act as a kangaroo pouch. Hide candy, stickers, animal crackers, and small plastic animals throughout the party area. The guests will hop around the party area and find the different objects to collect in their pouch.

Bird Without a Nest: Choose one child to be "it." This child is a bird without a nest. Divide the rest of the children into groups of three. (An extra person can be the caller.) Each group of three makes a bird in a nest, by two children facing each other and holding hands (the nest) and the third child (the bird) standing inside of their arms.

The caller yells "Find a nest!" and all the birds, including the one without a nest, have to run and find another nest. The bird left without a nest becomes "it."

Doggie, Doggie, Where's Your Bone? The birthday child will be the "Doggie" and will sit on a small chair with the party guests sitting behind him. Place a small object under his chair. (A dog bone would be ideal.) The Doggie will close his eyes. Silently choose a player to quietly go up and "steal" the Doggie's bone. That child will hide it from view.

The children then say, "Doggie, Doggie, where's your bone? Somebody took it from your home!" The Doggie will turn around, open his eyes, and try to guess who took his bone. Give him two guesses and then reveal who stole his bone. That person then becomes the Doggie. Continue the game until everyone has had a chance to be the Doggie and has stolen the bone.

Save the Animals: Choose one player to be the "hunter." The other party guests are the "animals." The hunter will chase the animals throughout the party area. When the hunter tags a running animal, the animal will begin to slowly sink to the ground. For the animal to be saved, another animal must tag him before he falls to the ground. If saved, he may continue the game as before. If no one has saved him and he has fallen to the ground, he then becomes a hunter and tries to capture the other animals.

Animal Clues: Divide the group into teams with three to four children per team. Each team will receive paper, markers, and a set of clues describing various animals.

To begin the game, one child from each team will read a clue to the team. This continues until the team has gathered enough clues to know which animal is being described. They will then draw the animal described in their clues. When the teams have completed their animals, they will show each other their drawings. Suggested clues:

a) I do not fly.
   I grow to four feet tall and
   weigh thirty-five pounds.
   I live in the Antarctic.
   My wings and webbed feet
   help me swim underwater.
   (*penguin*)

b) I like to eat thorny desert
   plants.
   I can drink twenty-seven
   gallons of water in ten
   minutes.
   I can carry heavy loads.
   I have humps on my back.
   (*camel*)

c) Hamburger meat comes from
   me.
   I have spots.
   I am a farm animal.
   A nutritious beverage comes
   from me.
   (*cow*)

d) I sleep standing up.
   I have spots.
   I have stubby horns covered in
   skin.
   I eat leaves from very tall trees.
   (*giraffe*)

e) I have four toes on my front
   paws.
   I have a cold, wet nose.
   I can be goofy, a lady, or a
   tramp.
   I am man's best friend.
   (*dog*)

f) I can be siamese, calico, or
   persian.
   My eyes glow in the dark.
   I like to hunt mice.
   I have nine lives.
   (*cat*)

King of the Jungle! This is a good wind down activity to play as you are waiting for the parents to come to pick up their children from the party.

Choose one player to be the hunter. The other children are the lions. The lions count to ten, while the hunter pretends to be asleep. After counting to ten the lions must "freeze." The hunter opens his eyes and tries to "catch" one of the lions moving. Once the hunter catches a lion that has moved, that lion helps the hunter catch other lions moving. The lion that stays still the longest becomes "King of the Jungle."

Mix-Up Party

INVITATIONS

• Fold a sheet of construction paper in half (see below). Cut out an outline of a person, with the feet on the fold line. With the fold line at the top (the person is upside down), write the invitation information on the inside. Describe the party theme on the outside by writing, "I'm all mixed up! Come to my party for a crazy day!" Be sure to address the envelopes upside down.

• Fold a sheet of construction paper in half. On the outside of the invitation, draw an upside down or silly scene. The party theme can be described on the invitation as shown below.

Suggest that the guests wear their clothes backwards or silly and wear two shoes that do not match. When they arrive say "Good-bye." When they leave say "Hello." Be ready to sing "You to Birthday Happy!"

DECORATIONS

1. Hang a "Happy Birthday, Amy!" banner upside down.
2. Place the candles in the sides of the birthday cake.
3. Attach a large cutout of the upside down person invitation to the front door. Write "EMOCLEW" across the cutout.
4. Make a poster stating the party "rules":

> Rule #1: In any photo taken of you, you must be making a silly face.
> Rule #2: Everyone must walk backwards at all times.
> Rule #3: The appropriate song is "You to Birthday Happy."
> Rule #4: Candles must be blown out before singing and wishes are made after blowing out the candles.
> Rule #5: Say "You Thank" to show appreciation.
> Rule #6: The last person in line will always go first and the first person last.
> Rule #7: Throughout the party, call everyone by their "backward" name.

Make name tags for everyone, written with the last (or middle) name first and the first name last. For older children, write everyone's first name spelled backward and have the guests call each other by this backwards name.

REFRESHMENTS

At a mix-up party the guests sit under the table to eat. To be backward, serve the dessert first and then the meal.

Clown Cake: Bake your favorite cake mix in one 9-inch square pan and one 9-inch round pan. Cut the square layer diagonally to make a large triangle to use for the clown's hat (see below). Cut the remainder of the layer into four triangles for the collar. Assemble and frost the clown

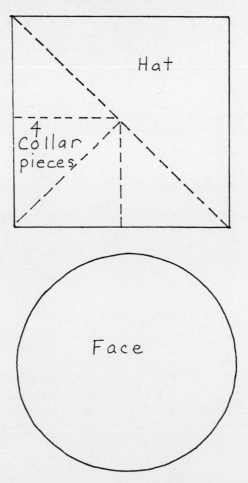

cake. Make a face on the round layer with gumdrops for eyes, a cherry nose, and red licorice laces to outline the mouth. Use sprinkles on the hat and collar. Use cherries or gumdrops for the pom-poms on the hat (see above).

Upside Down Ice Cream: Place one scoop of ice cream in a serving dish. Put a sugar cone on top of the ice cream and top with a cherry.

Inside Out Sandwiches: Serve sandwiches made with the bread in the middle and the luncheon meat on the outside.

Surprise Pops:

4 bananas	2 tablespoons milk
6 tablespoons cocoa	4 tablespoons honey
1 teaspoon vanilla extract	8 wooden craft sticks

Mix together the cocoa, vanilla, milk, and honey. Peel the bananas and cut them in half. Insert a stick into the flat (cut) end. Roll the bananas in the chocolate mixture. Put the bananas on waxed paper and freeze them overnight.

Crazy Drinks: Serve cans of soda or juice upside down by opening them on the bottom with a can opener.

Fruit Clowns: This clown is as much fun to make as it is to eat. Give each child one half of a green apple, placed flesh side down on a plate. (Dip apple slices in lemon juice to prevent browning.) Using peanut butter as "glue," attach cereals, cherries, raisins, and pineapple rings to the apple to make a clown face. Use a scoop of shredded cheese or carrots for the hair and a wedge of red apple for the hat. A bow tie can be made from two orange wedges and a cherry (see below).

PARTY FAVORS

• Line a 16-ounce plastic cup with coordinating colored plastic wrap and fill with party favors. Tie the wrap together at the top with matching ribbon.

• Let the children decorate their own **Crazy Party Favor Bags** (see Crafts on page 24).

• *Suggested favors:* puzzles, brain teasers, "What's wrong with this picture?" books, kaleidoscopes, Silly Putty, magic tricks, out-of-season treats or candy.

CRAFTS

Crazy Party Favor Bags: Give each child a plain white paper bag. Cut pieces of string into 18-inch lengths. Dip the string into paint and remove the excess. Lay the string on the bag in any desired design and press a paper towel over the string onto the bag. If desired, take another string, dip it into another color, and make a new design over the first color.

Silly Scenes: Let the children create their version of the silliest picture they can draw. Start them off with a few suggestions, such as the following:
- the sky on the bottom, the ground above
- a fish in a bird's nest
- flowers blooming at the bottom with stems on top
- a house with a chimney on the side, door in the roof
- people standing on their heads
- a car with square wheels

Balloon Faces:
  12-inch balloon
  pie tin
  miscellaneous decorations, such as markers, yarn, ribbon, buttons,
    pom-poms, tissue paper

Poke a hole in the center of the pie tin. Inflate the balloon and knot it. Invert the pie tin to form the "shoulders," and insert the knot of the balloon into the hole. Let the children decorate the faces on their balloons using the miscellaneous decorations.

Clowning Around: Paint a board to resemble a clown in a handstand position. Cut a circle from the board for the face. Take an instant photograph of each child with their face in the circle. Let the children make a picture frame for their clown photograph. Glue together four tongue depressors to make the frame and color it with markers.

GAMES

Backward Relay Races: Divide the guests into teams. In each race, the first child on each team will race across the party area, around a stationary object, and return to tag the next teammate in line. In each race, the children must be moving backward. *Examples*: Race one: the children are walking backward. Race two: they are jumping backward. Race three: backward "wheelbarrow" races.

Mixed-Up Pin on Game: In this silly version of "Pin the Tail on the Donkey," the children will take turns attaching their piece to an unrelated target. *Examples*: pin the ears on the car, pin the shoe on the fish, pin the elephant trunk on the donkey, etc. Any mixed-up combination will be fun.

Blindfold the child, give him a spin, and send him toward the target (a drawing on poster board). The piece must remain at the first spot he touches. It is fun to see the silly results.

Puzzle Relay: Divide the children into teams, with three or four children on a team. Provide one 25-piece puzzle for each team. Mix all the puzzle pieces together on a center table. Give each team its own table, equally spaced from the center.

To begin the relay, one child from each team will run to the center table and return with one puzzle piece, tagging the next teammate to run. As additional pieces are brought to the table, the teammates work together to assemble the puzzle. A piece belonging to a different puzzle must be returned to the center when the mistake is realized. The first team to complete its puzzle is the winner.

Old McDonald: The song "Old McDonald Had a Farm" brings lots of laughter when it is all mixed-up. Sit the children in a circle and begin the song. Each child will add a new animal and sound to begin each verse. However, it must be the wrong sound for that animal. *Examples*: the cow will "oink," the pig will "meow," the cat will "moo," etc.

Simon Says—So What! Preschoolers always enjoy a game of "Simon Says." However, at this party, we never do what Simon says, but only follow the commands of the speaker. Let the children take turns being Simon and acknowledge all who remember to play the opposite.

Mixed-Up Shoes: Divide the children into two teams and have them sit in two lines, facing each other. All children will remove their shoes and place them in a pile in the center of the two teams.

When the game begins, the first child in each line will run to the shoe pile, find one of his shoes, return to his place in line, and put on his shoe. When he has completed tying the shoe, the next child on his team will go find his shoe in the shoe pile. Play continues until each member of the team is wearing both of his shoes. The first team to finish is the winner.

Name Game: Randomly write letters of the alphabet on stickers. Have five stickers per child. Place all stickers into a bucket.

This is an outdoor game requiring a large plastic play ball and the space to run and throw. Assign each child a number. The children stand in a group as the birthday child throws the ball up into the air. While the ball is in the air, the child throwing it calls out a number. All the children run and scatter while the child with that number catches the ball. As soon as it is caught, all children must "freeze." The child with the ball is allowed to take up to three steps before throwing the ball at another player. If someone is hit by the throw, he goes to the bucket, picks out a letter, and sticks it to his shirt. That player is the next child to throw the ball into the air. Play continues, with children collecting a maximum of five stickers.

The five letters across the children's shirts become their "mix-up" name. Practice pronouncing them and call each other by these names for the rest of the party.

Mix-Up, May I? In this version of "Mother, May I?" the children will do the opposite of whatever step they have been given permission.

The children line up in a row across the starting line. The leader gives commands to each child in turn. ("Eric, take three giant steps.") The child must reply, "Mix-up, may I?" If he does, the leader says, "Yes, you may," and the child will do an opposite move (by taking three baby steps). If the child does not do an opposite move, or does not remember to first ask, "Mix-up, may I?" he returns to the starting line and his turn is over. The first child to cross the finish line wins.

Suggested steps: kangaroo jumps and bunny hops; umbrella (twirl) steps and scissors (crossover) steps; frog leaps and cricket hops; giant steps and baby steps; rabbit run and turtle walk.

Tic-Tac-Toe: Place nine large plastic cups snugly together in a square box (three rows of three). On his turn, the child will toss three plastic balls into the cups. Because this is a mix-up party, the goal is NOT to achieve three in a row. Any configuration in the cups that does not align is a winner.

Mix-Up Party Favors: Seat the children in a circle. Each child will have a bag filled with one kind of party favor totaling the same number as there are guests. Make sure the outsides of the bags are identical. *Example:* If 10 children are present, you will need one bag with 10 balloons, one bag with 10 markers, one bag with 10 lollipops, etc.

Explain that at this mix-up party a mistake was made and the party favors are not mixed. The goal of this game is to mix-up the favors so that everyone has only one each of the prizes.

While playing music, the guests randomly trade bags with each other. When the music stops, each child takes one item from the bag and puts it in her lap as long as it is not a duplicate. Keep playing the trading until everyone has one each of all the party favor items. As bags are emptied eliminate them from the circle.

Environmental Party

INVITATIONS

● Cut the invitation from a brown grocery bag. Draw the recycle symbol (three arrows forming a triangle) and describe the environmental theme in the invitation.

● Send a circular invitation, decorated like a globe (see below). Describe on the invitation the "Save the Earth" theme of the party. If appropriate, ask the guests to wrap their gifts in newspaper or to reuse other packaging for wrapping paper.

DECORATIONS

1. A candleholder centerpiece can be made using an empty 2-liter soda bottle (see right). The children can also make these candleholders as a craft.

For each candleholder, cut the top off an empty 2-liter bottle directly above the label. Cut a 6-inch circle from poster board. Place a bunch of artificial flowers in the center of the circle and top with the "dome" end of the soda bottle. Use a hot-melt glue gun to secure the dome in place. Tie ribbon into a

bow and secure to the spout of the bottle. Insert a 10-inch tapered candle.

2. Cut large letters from newspapers or paper bags to display the message "Happy 10th Birthday, David" in the party area.

3. Decorate with pictures of endangered animals.

Note: We do not recommend using balloons to decorate at this party since they can be harmful to the environment.

REFRESHMENTS

Earth Cake: Decorate a round layer cake to resemble the earth. Use green frosting to draw the continents and blue frosting for the oceans.

Snowballs and Sludge Balls:

1 cup crunchy peanut butter
¼ cup margarine, softened
2 cups toasted rice cereal
1 cup powdered sugar

8 ounces chocolate candy coating (for sludge balls)
8 ounces white candy coating (for snowballs)
2 tablespoons shortening

Combine peanut butter and margarine in a large bowl. Add cereal and powdered sugar until evenly combined. Roll mixture into bite-sized balls and set aside.

Using a microwave or a double boiler, melt the chocolate coating and one tablespoon shortening. Repeat with the white coating. Dip each peanut butter ball into one coating and place on a waxed paper lined tray. Drizzle with melted white or chocolate. Refrigerate until firm. Makes two dozen snowballs and two dozen sludge balls.

Earth-Wiches: Cut 48 slices of white bread into 4-inch circles. Spread catsup or mayonnaise on top of 24 slices of bread. Top with 4-inch round slices of luncheon meats and 4-inch circles of cheese. Top with remaining bread cutouts. Garnish with carrot sticks or slices of fresh fruit.

Global Pizza:

10 mini bagels, split and toasted
15 ounce jar pizza sauce

½ cup chopped pepperoni or Canadian bacon
8 ounces shredded mozzarella cheese

On each bagel spread one tablespoon of the sauce. Top with the meat and cheese. Broil for 3 to 4 minutes, until the cheese melts or bake at 350 degrees for 15 minutes. Makes 20 mini pizzas.

Note: When serving refreshments use only washable dishes and flatware. Avoid snacks with individual packaging.

PARTY FAVORS

- Use reusable containers, such as canvas shopping bags or pencil boxes for the goody bags.
- Cover an empty can with wallpaper and glue in place. Fill with treats.
- *Suggested favors:* posters, pictures, or stickers of animals; *Planet-3* magazine; seed packets; tree seedlings; natural snacks, such as raisins or sunflower seeds; *50 Simple Things Kids Can Do to Save the Earth* published by the Earthworks Press.

CRAFTS

Eco-Airplanes: To make each toy airplane you will need two foam trays and a paper clip. Cut a plane body shape (side view), wings, and a tailpiece from the foam trays (see below). Cut slits into the body of the plane to slide in the wings and tailpiece. Add the paper clip to the nose of the plane for balance. Decorate the plane with markers.

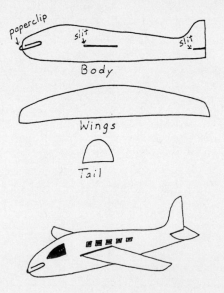

Save-a-Tree Napkins: For each napkin, cut a 15" × 15" square from a white bed sheet or other soft, clean fabric. Carefully pull threads from the edges to make fringe. Give each child a set of four napkins and let him decorate the napkins with fabric markers.

Newspaper Party Hats: Fold a sheet of newspaper in half (see below). Bring the top two corners to meet in the center and fold into place. Fold up the bottom edges on each side to form the brim and tape together at the ends.

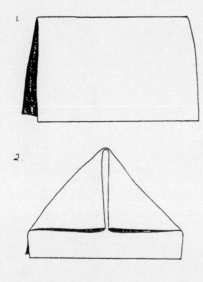
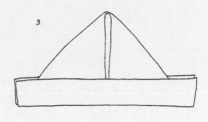

Recycled Products Bird Feeder:

1 2-liter plastic soda bottle with cap
1 6-inch margarine tub lid
wire
birdseed

Pry off the black bottom portion of the plastic bottle (see right). Cut a hole in the center of the plastic lid. Invert the 2-liter bottle and fit the lid snugly over the neck of the bottle. Cut small holes in the dome of the bottle, near the neck, to drop the seeds onto the lid. Slit the top of the feeder and insert the wire through the slits to make a hanger. Decorate the feeders with permanent markers. Send the children home with a bag of seeds to fill their feeders.

Natural Bird Feeder: Tie a long yarn loop securely to a large pinecone. Spread a thin layer of peanut butter over the pinecone. Roll the pinecone in birdseed until it is completely covered. Wrap the bird feeder in waxed paper to take home.

GAMES

Endangered Animal Game: Tape pictures of endangered animals on sticks and mount sticks into the ground. Encircle each animal with a large hoop or string.

Divide the group into two teams. Call team one the "Polluters" (P's) and team two the "Savers" (S's). Each team member will have a beanbag to toss. The "P" team has beanbags made to resemble litterbugs. The "S" team tosses sunshine beanbags.

All children will stand a premarked distance away from each animal and throw their beanbags, trying to land them inside the circle. After all children have tossed, count the bags each team has landed in the circle. If there are more "S's" than "P's"—the animal lives and stays standing. If there are more "P's" than "S's"—the animal dies and you will lay the sign down on the ground. After completing the animal stations, count how many animals were polluted and how many were saved to determine which team is the winner.

Gallon Scoop Toss: Make a scoop for each child using an empty plastic gallon milk jug (see below). Lay the jug on its side with the handle up. Cut away the bottom of the jug and the upper side below the handle.

Place the children into two lines facing each other about four feet apart. The children in line "A" will toss balls to the children they are facing in line "B" who will catch the balls in their scoops. After each catch, each child takes one step backward and tosses again. Continue tossing the ball back and forth. Pairs are eliminated if they drop the ball. The pair that successfully tosses and catches from the farthest distance is the winner.

The "litterbug" and "sunshine" beanbags (see **Endangered Animal Game** above) can be tossed instead of balls.

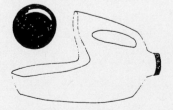

Sweep Up the Litter: Divide the guests into teams of three children per team. Each team will need one broom, one large shovel, one trash bag, and 15 empty soda cans.

The first player sweeps the cans into the shovel, being held by the second player. The second player empties the shovel into the trash bag being held by the third player. The first team with the 15 cans in the bag is the winner.

Shoot Pollution: The children will stand in two lines facing each other about eight feet apart. Cover the face of each child in line "A" with shaving cream. Give each child in line "B" a loaded water gun. The first child to shoot all the cream off of her partner is the winner.

Pass the Trash: Divide the guests into teams. Each team will stand in a row with about a two-foot space between the teammates. At the beginning of each team's line is a pile of empty soda cans. At the end of each line is a trash can or recycling bin. The first player in each line runs up to the pile of cans, picks up one can, and runs backward to his starting position. He will throw the can between his legs to the second player who passes it over his shoulder to the third player. The play continues under and over. The last player in line throws the can into the recycling bin and runs to the front of the line. The first team to have all the soda cans in the bin is the winner.

Rolling Relay: Divide the children into two teams. Each team has one large, round, empty trash can. String or mark off two lanes across the party area approximately three feet wide. Each player on the team must roll the trash can on its rim to the end of the lane and back. The first team to have all of its players complete the relay wins.

Shoot to Win: Divide the group into two teams. Give team one a tub of soap bubbles. Each child on that team will use plastic six-pack rings to blow bubbles over the party area. Give each child on team two a loaded water gun. Their mission is to shoot the bubbles before any of them hit the ground. After a few minutes of play, have the teams switch roles so everyone will have a chance to make bubbles and to shoot.

Trash Bag Relay: Divide the guests into teams. Each team will need two shovels and a large trash bag filled with newspapers or plastic containers that has been fastened securely closed. To begin the relay, two players from each team will pick up the shovels and scoop up the trash bag. Together they will run, carrying the bag, to the opposite end of the party area, lay down the shovels and run back. The next two players will run, pick up the shovels, scoop up the trash bag, and bring it back to the starting line. This continues until all players on the team have had a turn. The first team to finish is the winner.

Toss the Trash: For this game you will need labeled recycling bins and emptied recyclable items. Stand the opened recycling bins along a wall. Scatter the recyclable items around the room.

Divide the group into two teams. To begin, one player from each team runs into the littered area. Each player picks up one piece of litter and determines in which box it belongs. From the spot where the player picked up the litter, he must toss it into the correct bin. If he misses, he tries again until it is in the bin. After it is in, he goes back to his team and tags the next player. Play continues until all of the litter is saved for recycling.

Save the Earth: Make five signs to represent the stations in this game: 1) Grocery Store, 2) Lake, 3) Forest, 4) Garden, 5) Endangered Kingdom. The items the children collect during the game can be used as party favors.

Divide the group into two teams. The first person on each team must do the following:

a) Go the Grocery Store and put his "purchases" into a reusable canvas or cloth bag. (Each child puts 2 or 3 candy or snack items into his own bag.)
b) Visit the Lake and remove three things that do not belong there. (The lake can be a small pool or tub filled with novelty items such as balls, shoes, cans, etc.)
c) Go to the Forest and stand up the trees that have been cut down. (These are paper trees which are lying on the ground.)
d) "Plant" seeds to beautify the Garden. (Hide seeds under a piece of brown fabric.)
e) Return an endangered animal to the Forest. (Pick up a toy animal from the Endangered Kingdom and return it to the Forest.)

After the child completes his round of earth saving tasks, he returns to the start and the next child will begin. Continue until each child has had a chance to "Save the Earth."

Earth Puzzle: Make two large puzzles of the earth to be used as scorecards, by gluing pictures of the earth to sturdy cardboard and cutting the cardboard into 10 jigsaw puzzle pieces.

Divide the children into two teams. Alternate asking each team a question concerning the environment. When a team gives a correct answer it receives a piece of the earth. The first team to finish the puzzle wins the game.

Listed below are suggested questions. You may wish to make these multiple-choice questions, or true and false questions. They include many interesting facts that you may wish to share with the children even if you do not play this game.

a) What is the correct way to dispose of six-pack holders? (Snip each circle with scissors before tossing into the trash to save animals that may become trapped in them.)

b) Name an alternative to plastic wrap and aluminum foil. (reusable airtight containers or waxed paper which is biodegradable.)

c) How can we eliminate the use of paper towels? (Use cloth rags to wipe up spills, then wash and reuse the rags.)

d) How much water runs out of the tap each minute? (three to five gallons)

e) Why use a phosphate free detergent? (Phosphates cause "algae bloom" which uses up the oxygen in the water that plants and marine life need.)

f) How can you save water when washing the dishes? (Filling the basin uses five gallons of water. Running the tap uses over 30 gallons.)

g) What kind of bag should you carry purchases in? (If it is a small purchase do not take a bag; otherwise, use washable reusable canvas bags.)

h) What is the life span of a rechargeable battery? (Rechargeables last approximately four years.)

i) How long will an aluminum can last? (One can will litter the earth 500 years.)

j) What is a landfill? (an area designated for trash and garbage, also called a dump.)

k) What does EPA stand for? (Environmental Protection Agency)

l) How much water do you use to brush your teeth? (If the water is running, you will use over five gallons of water. If you wet and rinse your brush, you will only use a half gallon.)

m) How many trees do you use a year? (Every American uses seven trees a year.)

n) Which uses more gasoline, to stop and restart your car at every stop or to let your car idle? (Letting your car idle is less efficient than restarting it after about one minute.)

o) How many gallons of water are used in the toilet? (five to seven gallons with each flush)

p) What should you do with your Christmas tree after Christmas? (Take it to participating parks or natural resource departments who will turn it into mulch.)

q) What are the three R's needed to protect our earth? (reduce, reuse, and recycle)

r) What are the safest kinds of paint, markers, and glue? (waterbased)

s) How many hours can you use your TV on the energy saved from recycling one aluminum can? (three hours)

t) How many garbage trucks does the United States fill each day? (63,000)
u) How many foam cups are thrown away each year? (25 billion)
v) Which are the best crayons to use? (Crayons made of beeswax do not contain the oil found in other crayons.)
w) How many trees does it take to print a newspaper? (Each week it takes an entire forest of over 500,000 trees to supply America with the Sunday newspaper.)
x) Which is a better purchase, a biodegradable item or an item that is recyclable? (Biodegradable items require many years of sunlight to decompose. They will not receive sunlight in a landfill. Recycling saves resources now.)
y) What is the recyclable symbol? (three arrows forming a triangle)
z) Name something you can do to save the earth. (Accept any reasonable answer.)

Olympic Party

INVITATIONS

• Fold a piece of yellow construction paper and cut out a circle, being careful not to cut on the fold line. On the outside of the invitation write "Go for the Gold!" (see below). On the inside, write all necessary party information. Punch a hole in the top and insert a red, white, and blue ribbon.

• On white paper, the size of your envelope, draw the five rings representing the Olympic symbol and color them (left to right) blue, yellow, black, green, and red (see below). Inside each ring write the party information.

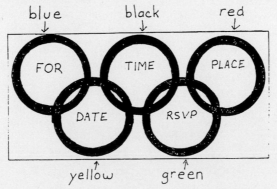

DECORATIONS

1. Use poster board to make flags representing different countries.
2. Make a torch holder for the **Olympic Torches** (see Crafts, page 39). Invert a cardboard box (or strong lid) and cut holes in it approximately two inches in diameter.
3. Make an Olympic flag using a large white paper tablecloth. Draw the Olympic symbol on the flag. Roll the flag and use it during the **Opening Ceremony** (see Games, page 39).

REFRESHMENTS

Stars and Stripes Cake: Prepare a white or yellow cake mix in a 9"×13" pan. Spread with one 8-ounce tub of thawed whipped topping. Create the design of the United States flag by placing ⅓ cup of blueberries in the top left-hand corner, to represent the stars, and halved strawberries in rows for the stripes. Refrigerate at least one hour before serving.

Olympic Cookies: Prepare a sugar cookie recipe. Roll the dough to ⅛-inch thickness. Cut the dough into 2-inch rings. Interlock five rings to form the shape of the Olympic symbol. Add colored sugars and bake according to directions.

The United States Pizza: Prepare your favorite homemade pizza recipe and place on a cookie sheet. Design the shape of the United States flag on the pizza with black olives for the stars and slices of pepperoni for the stripes.

Energy Mix: Melt ¾ cup peanut butter in a microwave and pour over 9 cups of assorted Chex cereals. Spread onto a cookie sheet and bake in a preheated oven at 300 degrees for 15 minutes. Place the mixture in a large plastic bag with powdered sugar and shake until the mixture is coated. Serve in individual bags.
Optional: Add one cup milk chocolate chips or one cup raisins.

PARTY FAVORS

• Use the **Olympic Torches** (see Crafts, page 39) as your favor bags. Place energy bars, such as candy bars or granola bars, inside of each torch.

• Decorate a white lunch bag with blue stars and red stripes to create a "flag bag." Fill it with frisbees, jump ropes, balls, flags, etc.

CRAFTS

Olympic Sash: Prepare for the events by making sashes to wear, which represent the country for which the child is competing (see below).

These can be made from wide ribbon or cotton fabric. Write the name of a country on each sash and a number on the back. Give the children fabric markers and stickers to use in decorating their "Olympic Sash."

Olympic Torches: For each torch, curl a 10-inch paper plate to form a cone (see above). Staple or tape it closed. Attach red and orange crepe paper streamers at the top of the cone to represent the flames.

Olympic Medals: Cut a 4-inch circle from yellow poster board for a gold medal. Punch a hole in the top of the medal. Insert a 28-inch red, white, and blue ribbon through the hole and tie the ends together.

Attach star stickers to the medal, as an award, for completing each activity. At the end of the party, each guest will have a medal covered with colorful stars as a keepsake.

GAMES

Opening Ceremony: Give each guest a sash, torch, and medal (see Crafts, above). Parade the "Olympians" around the course. Each child will stop and place his torch in the holder to make one large flame.

Beginning with the birthday child, the children will raise their arms and unroll the Olympic flag (see Decorations, page 38) above their heads. Everyone will have a chance to touch the flag for good luck.

When the ceremony is completed announce, "Let the Games Begin!"

Gymnastics: This activity encourages creativity. Section off an area where the "gymnasts" will compete. This can be done with crepe paper or rope. You can use a large blanket as a substitute for the mat. Include background music to be played during the routines.

Inform each contestant that he should include in the one minute routine a spin, jump, handstand, cartwheel and split. Give one star sticker for each requirement included in the routine.

Balance Beam: Place a two-by-four on the ground. State the required exercises the gymnasts are to incorporate into their routine. Set the timer for 30 seconds and give them one star for each requirement that is met.

Boxing: Use an inflated bop bag which is weighted at the bottom. Set the timer for 30 seconds and count how many times the child knocks the bop bag down.

The Long Jump: Stand each contestant 15 feet from a predetermined line. He will take a running start toward the line, and will jump as far as he can. On the sideline, mark the distance jumped with a stick inserted into the ground. Give each contestant two tries.

The Broad Jump: The contestant will stand on a line and jump from a stationary position. Give each contestant two tries and mark the farthest distance jumped by inserting a stick on the sideline.

The High Jump: Insert two poles into the ground and attach a crepe paper streamer from pole to pole. Each contestant will jump over the crepe paper. Raise the paper each time the contestants successfully clear the streamer.

The Javelin Throw: A wrapping paper roll will make a safe javelin. Give each guest two tries at throwing the javelin. The child who throws it the farthest is the winner.

The Disc Throw: Using a plastic disc, demonstrate the correct way to hold the disc. Give each child two tries to throw it as far as he can.

100-Meter Run: The runners will race around a "track." Keep a record of their times. Set up a table with cups of water for the runners to drink or splash on their faces.

Hurdling: To make a hurdle, insert two poles into the ground, spaced about two feet apart. Attach a crepe paper streamer from pole to pole. The guests will run a race while jumping over the hurdles.

Pseudo-Swimming Relay: Divide the guests into teams. The first player on each team will imitate a swimming stroke, such as the breast-stroke, while running across the yard and back. He will tag the second player who will imitate the butterfly stroke, and so forth. Continue with the backstroke and the sidestroke. The first team to finish is the winner.

Equestrian Course: This course can be a racing event against another player or a timed event. Instruct each contestant to gallop on a stick horse around a race track. The track may include cones to run around, hurdles to jump over, or gates to run through.

Cycling: Contestants will ride on small bikes in a circle and in and out of cones. Supply cups of water for them to pour on themselves or for drinking purposes.

Jump Roping: Count the number of successful jumps to rank the winners. Older children could be rated on special jumps, such as touching the ground, jumping on one foot, or moving in and out of the rope.

Bobsled Relay: Using skateboards for bobsleds, the first child on each team will sit on the "bobsled" and use his feet to scoot the sled along the course. When he crosses the finish line, the next player on the team begins. The first team to finish is the winner.

Figure Skating Relay: For each team, draw a skating pattern with chalk. The first person on each team will slide her feet along the pattern. When she returns to the start, the second child will "skate" the pattern, and so forth. Anyone caught running must skate backward for the remainder of the course. The first team to finish is the winner.

The Closing Ceremony: Stand the children in a line. Let the birthday child hold the American flag and have all the children sing the "National Anthem." If the children do not know this song, you may wish to have them say the "Pledge of Allegiance." Congratulate the children on the number of stars they have earned on their medals.

Carnival Party

The Carnival Party will keep a large group of children involved in a variety of activities.

Plan to have six to eight booths at your party. You will need one adult helper for every two booths. Award small, trinket-type prizes at each booth. Plan to have approximately ten small prizes per child. Vary the prizes at each booth. For older children, award tickets. When they have collected a required number of tickets, they will exchange them for a prize.

At the beginning of the carnival, give the children bags with handles to carry all the "loot" they are going to win. Label each bag with a child's name to avoid any mix-ups with prizes. Give name tags to each guest to assist the adults working the booths. Explain to the children that they may go to any booth at any time. They decide where they play and how often.

Plan on playing at the booths for approximately one hour. After you have completed the booths and distributed all the prizes, bring the group together for refreshments.

INVITATIONS

• Draw a picture of a clown juggling balls (see illustration A, page 43). Write the party information in the balls. If desired, instruct the children to color the invitation and bring it to the party for a coloring contest.

• Use colored construction paper to make a triple-dip ice cream cone (see illustration B, page 43). Write on it "Come to Julie's Birthday Carnival for a Cool Time" followed by the party information.

A

B

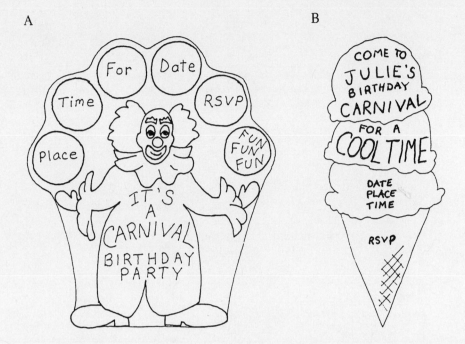

DECORATIONS

1. Divide the party area into booths using small stakes, string, and crepe paper (see below). Insert the stakes into the ground. Tie the string from stake to stake at the top and the bottom. Wrap the crepe paper streamers up and down around the string to create a colorful divider for each booth. Accent the booths with balloons.

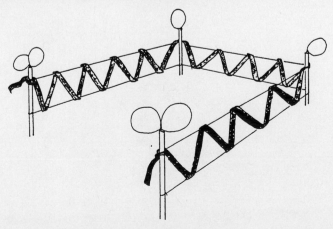

2. Decorate each booth entrance with a sign stating the name of the booth and briefly explaining the rules of that activity. Be sure to specify how many chances each contestant is allowed during a turn.

3. The entrance to the carnival can be made special by creating an archway of balloons. Attach a string across the top of the entrance and tie balloons to the string.

REFRESHMENTS

Sucker Pull Birthday Cake: This colorfully decorated cake is also a party game. Frost your favorite cake. Purchase one sucker for every child. Mark the bottoms of half of the sucker sticks with a marker. Insert all the suckers into the cake. Let each child pull a sucker out of the cake. All children will keep their suckers and those with marked sticks will win extra prizes.

Ice Cream Clowns:

sugar cones   maraschino cherries
vanilla ice cream   chocolate chips
decorative colored frosting

Place one scoop of ice cream on a plate for the clown's head. Turn one cone upside down and place it on the ice cream for the hat. Use chocolate chips for the eyes and mouth, and a cherry for the nose. Decorate with frosting to make a collar and decorations on the hat. Attach a cherry to the top of the hat with frosting (see below).

Sno-Cones: For each flavor of syrup combine the following:

1 envelope unsweetened   1 cup sugar
  drink mix   ½ cup water

Store, refrigerated, in a plastic squirt bottle.
To serve, saturate a cup of crushed or shaved ice with the syrup.

Picnic Lunch: Prepare individual lunch bags filled with sandwiches, fruit, popcorn, peanuts or cotton candy. The children will grab a bag and a drink from the cooler and enjoy their lunches together.

BOOTHS

Hook a Prize: Wrap prizes individually. Tape ribbon across the top of the prizes to create two large loops. Attach a piece of string approximately three feet long to a stick or pole. Tie a plastic hook on the end of the string.

Place the prizes in an empty swimming pool or tub and have the children try to "Hook a Prize."

Fortune Teller: A "Fortune Teller" will forecast each child's future. Offer an assortment of objects (see below). Each object represents one forecast. The fortune teller will instruct the child to pick three objects and will base her prediction on the objects selected. Use a "magic mirror" or "crystal ball" as a prop to see into the future. *Examples:*

ring—will be happily married
thimble—is very creative
toy train—will travel frequently
ball—will be good at sports
coin—will be rich
flower—will be surrounded with beauty
music note—will become a rock 'n' roll star

Egg Surprise: Place small prizes in plastic eggs. Place the eggs in a tub of water. The children will "fish" for their prizes using a small fish net or slotted spoon.

Guess How Many? Fill a clear jar with small pieces of candy. Count the candy and write the amount in a secret place. The children will write down how many pieces they think are in the jar. The child who is closest to the correct number wins the candy.

Bumper Race Cars: Nail one nail in each corner of a rectangular board. Place two strong rubber bands across the two nails at each end. Draw two dotted lines across the board approximately three inches from each rubber band. Each child will push a plastic toy car into the rubber band with just enough force to make the car rebound into the other rubber band. The goal is to get the car to stop between the two dotted lines, without touching or overlapping the lines (see below).

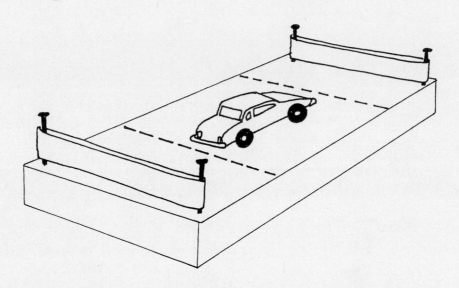

Candy Hunt: Cut a 9-inch hole in a box. Place foam packing peanuts and pieces of wrapped candy the same size as the peanuts into the box. Each child will reach in the box and remove three pieces of candy without looking.

Hoop a Prize: Nail four plastic bowls to a board. Place one prize in each bowl. The children will throw embroidery hoops around the bowls. If the hoop lands around the bowl, the child will keep that prize.

Pitching Pennies: Fill a small swimming pool or tub with water. Float two plastic lids from margarine containers on top of the water. Give each child three pennies. The children will try to throw the pennies onto the lid from a distance of about three feet. If the pennies land on a lid, the child wins a prize.

Coffee Can Catch: Nail three coffee cans, graduating in size, to a long board. The children will try to toss three beanbags into the cans. Offer different prizes for each size can. If tickets are being used, the number of tickets received should increase as the size of the cans decreases.

Soda Can Toss: Pyramid six empty soda cans on an inverted box. The children will toss a beanbag trying to knock over the cans. Be sure to mark off the distance each child should stand from the target. As they succeed, increase the distance from the target to increase the challenge.

Toss and Win. Attach an empty egg carton to the top of an inverted cardboard box. Each contestant will toss three small balls into the carton. If she is successful with one or more balls, she will win a prize.
Variation: Paint the egg cups to match colored balls. Prizes are awarded when balls are tossed into their matching cups.

Disc Throw: Insert a pole into the ground (see below). Attach a Hula Hoop to the top of the pole. The contestants will stand approximately eight to ten feet away and try to throw a plastic disc through the hoop to win a prize.

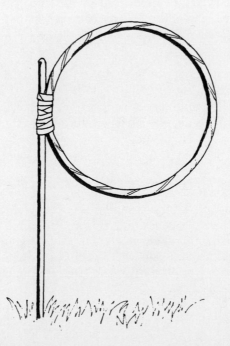

Wet Sponge Toss: Make a target which will be durable when wet by using plywood or a plastic tablecloth. Cut a 12-inch hole in the center of the target. Mark the distance the children should stand from the target and place a bucket of water at that distance. Give the contestant three sponges. The contestant will soak the sponges and try to toss them through the hole in the target.

A fun variation for older children is to have a volunteer stand behind the target and put his face into the hole. The children will toss wet sponges at his face.

First Aid Tent: Attach sheets to the top of a swing set to form a tent or use one of the booths. Equip the tent with bandages, wraps, slings, crutches, and waterbase acrylic paints. Paint the children with blood, stitches, or black eyes. Apply bandages to the children for head injuries, broken arms or legs, cuts, or bruises.

Face Painting: Offer the children a choice from six to eight different examples. Using waterbase acrylic paint and small brushes, paint the design on their cheeks or on the back of their hands.

Tic-Tac-Toe: Place nine large plastic cups snugly together in a square box (three rows of three). Give each contestant three plastic balls. The contestants will toss the balls into the cups, trying to get "Tic-Tac-Toe" (three in a row, any direction).

Squirt the Balloon: Hang a clothesline and attach clothespins along the line. Clip an inflated balloon to each clothespin. Mark a spot on the ground with tape or chalk for contestants to stand. From that spot each contestant will try to shoot a balloon with a water gun (or toss a beanbag at the balloon). If he hits a balloon, he wins a prize.

Birthday Gift Walk: Decorate paper plates with each guest's name and place them on the ground in a circle. The children will march around the circle as music is being played. When the music stops, have the birthday child look to see which name is printed on the plate where she is standing. That person will give his gift to the birthday child. Remove that plate from the circle and begin the music to continue the "Birthday Gift Walk."

Variation: All plates are the same except one which has a large star on the top. When the music stops, the guest by the star wins and gets to select a prize.

Water Balloon Toss: For the grand finale, have a water balloon toss. This activity brings everyone together and cools everyone on a hot day.

Prepare the water balloons prior to the party, with a minimum of four to five balloons per child.

Form two lines with partners facing each other. Each child will toss a water balloon to his partner, trying not to break it. If successful, both partners take one step backward and the balloon is tossed back to the first partner. When the water balloon breaks, that pair is out of the game. The game continues until there is only one pair remaining.

After the official water balloon toss is over, give the children the remaining water balloons for a water balloon fight.

Baby Doll Party

INVITATIONS

- With a permanent marker, write the invitation information on small cloth baby bibs and mail one to each guest.
- Cut two sheets of construction paper into the shape of a dollhouse (see below). On sheet one (the top sheet), cut three sides of the windows and door. The fourth side is a fold line. Glue sheet one to sheet two (the bottom sheet) around the outside edges only. Fold open the windows and door and write the invitation information inside.

Cut on dotted lines only

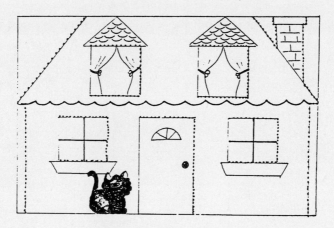

- Cut construction paper into the shape of a baby bottle. Write the invitation information on the ounce lines.

DECORATIONS

1. Place stuffed animals and dolls around the room.
2. Stack large alphabet building blocks in the party area. Blocks can

be made from cardboard boxes. With primary colors, paint capital letters on all sides of the boxes.

3. Place nursery items, such as a baby bathtub, changing table, stroller, swing, and walker around the party area.

4. For a centerpiece, tie three baby bottles together with a pastel, satin ribbon (tie into a bow) (see right). Partially fill the bottles with water. Insert one or two stems of fresh flowers in each bottle. Accent the table with baby rattles and small baby toys.

5. Make **Baby Cribs** from cardboard boxes (see Crafts, page 53).

REFRESHMENTS

Alphabet Block Cake: Bake your favorite cake mix in two 9-inch square pans. When completely cooled, layer the cake and cut it into four squares. Frost all squares with vanilla frosting. Use primary colored frostings to decorate the squares like alphabet blocks (see below). Arrange the cakes on a serving tray and accent with small wooden blocks around the tray.

Tea Party: Play "Tea Party" with the "moms" and baby dolls. Place bibs on the dolls. Serve mini-cupcakes on toy-sized dishes.

Mother and Daughter Banquet: Serve adult-size refreshments for the "moms" at the party, and serve child-size portions for their babies. *Suggestions:*

a) hot dogs for the moms and cocktail weiners for the babies
b) orange slices and mandarin oranges
c) large scoops and melon-ball sized scoops of ice cream
d) apples and applesauce
e) soda and juice

Baby Doll Cookies: Prepare your favorite sugar cookie recipe. Roll the dough to ⅛-inch thickness on a floured surface. Cut dough with a girl-shaped cookie cutter and bake.

Offer a variety of frostings and candies for each guest to decorate her own baby doll cookie (see below).

— stick of gum cut lengthwise
— yellow sugar hair
— silver ball eyes
— lace licorice
— large wafer candy cut in half
— cake decorations
— icing
— sprinkles
— chocolate chips

PARTY FAVORS

- Place candy treats inside baby food jars.
- Fill baby bottles with necessities for the babies, such as cotton balls, soap, washcloths, cotton swabs, or lotion.

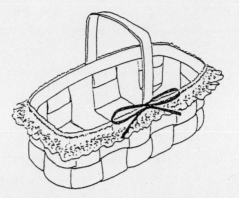

- Glue eyelet lace around the tops of small wicker baskets to form bassinets (see above). Decorate with a bow and fill with treats.
- Give each guest a "diaper bag" (gift tote bag) filled with a bottle, bib, pacifier, rattle, diaper, blanket, etc.

CRAFTS

Baby Crib: Prepare one crib for each child's baby doll using white cardboard computer boxes (see below). Cut 1-inch vertical strips on two opposite sides of the box to resemble crib slats.

From a coloring book, find pictures of teddy bears, dolls, bunnies, clowns, etc. Photocopy two pictures for every child.

As the children arrive at the party, have them color the pictures, cut them out, and glue them to the outside ends of the cribs. The children may also draw their own pictures on the ends of the cribs for decoration.

Mobiles: To make a mobile for the "Baby Crib," each child will need the following items:

    1 wooden dowel or plastic tube cut two inches longer than the width of the crib

    4 small baby toys or cardboard cutouts of animals

    4 pieces of curling ribbon or string

Tie one ribbon to each baby toy. Use a hole punch to make a small hole in the top center of the crib rails. Insert the dowel through the holes. Tie the ribbons to the dowel, hanging the toys low enough for the doll babies to play with them.

Baby Wrap: Prepare a baby wrap by cutting a fabric rectangle approximately 22" × 36" (see below). Fold to form a 12-inch pocket and stitch the edges together. Trim with rickrack, eyelet or lace.

Give the guests fabric markers to decorate the wrap for their babies. Suggest personalizing with their doll's name. Tuck the babies inside the pocket and rock them or lay them in their cribs for a nap.

Variation: Trim a 15-inch square of fabric with eyelet or lace. Decorate with fabric markers and use as a baby blanket.

fold

Baby Bibs: Cut semicircles of white fabric. Bind the edge by encasing it in double-fold bias tape and sew, extending each end of the tape 12 inches for the ties.

Give the guests fabric markers to decorate the bibs for their babies. Suggest personalizing the bib with their doll's name.

GAMES

Dress the Baby: Collect an assortment of infant and newborn baby items. Be sure to have enough to outfit each guest's baby.

Hide all the objects around the party area. Give each child a small shopping bag and a list of the objects she must find for her baby. Be sure everyone's list has the same number of items to find. *Example:*

1 shirt	1 rattle
1 pair of pants	1 blanket
2 socks	2 barrettes
2 shoes or booties	1 ribbon

When the game begins, the children must hunt and find everything on the list. Once they have found all the items on the list, they must dress their babies. The first child to dress her baby is the winner. Remind them not to pick up any additional items that are not on their lists and not to duplicate any items.

Suggestion: Be sure to note on the invitation the size of the doll you wish the guests to bring, so that the clothes you hide will fit the dolls at the party. You may wish to have several extra dolls on hand to be sure all children have the correct size.

Stroller Relay: The following items are needed for each team:

1 bib	1 burp cloth
1 pacifier on string	1 diaper bag
1 stroller	

To begin the race the first child on each team must do the following: put the bib under the doll's chin, hang the pacifier around the doll's neck, place the doll in the stroller, cover her left shoulder with the burp cloth, put the diaper bag over her right shoulder.

While carrying the diaper bag, the child must push the stroller across the party area, go around a stationary object at the opposite end, go back to start, and remove the five things that she has placed on herself and her doll. The next child will put all of the items on, and the race continues until each child on the team runs the course. The first team to finish is the winner.

Stack the Blocks: Divide the children into two teams. Place two tables on the opposite side of the party area. Place approximately twelve blocks on each table. As the game begins, the first child on each team runs to the table and stacks one block on another. She runs back and tags the second child who will run, stack up a third block, and return. The game continues until one team has successfully stacked all of its blocks.

Diaper the Baby: Divide the guests into teams. Set up a table for each team with baby wipes, powder, and diapers. When the game begins, the first child on each team must wipe, powder, and diaper her baby. When finished, the next child may begin. The team that completely diapers all its babies first wins.

As the children are diapering their babies, have the other guests sing this song to the tune of "London Bridge Is Falling Down":
"Change my little baby's pants
baby's pants, baby's pants.
Change my little baby's pants
all day long!"

Crawling Relay: Divide the group into teams. The first person on each team must crawl across the floor and back while holding her baby. She then tags the next child to begin. The first team to complete the relay wins.

Extra challenge: The children must push a block or a baby toy across the floor while crawling without using their hands.

Feed the Baby: Pair off the guests and have them sit facing each other. Each guest should have a baby food jar filled with small candy treats and a small spoon. The children then feed each other the candy. The first team that finishes the treats wins.

Lullaby Time: This would be a good activity to end the party or for laying the babies down for a nap while the "mothers" are busy with other activities.

As each mom is holding and rocking her baby, read aloud a short bedtime story. The moms can sing "Rock-a-Bye Baby" or "Twinkle, Twinkle Little Star" and put their sleeping babies in their cribs. Cover the babies with blankets and whisper "Shh!"

Dress Up Party

INVITATIONS

Specify on your invitations that this is a dress up party and everyone should wear her fanciest clothes. Be sure to inform everyone that this does not mean her best clothes, but her make-believe dress up clothes.

• Cut the hat pattern shown from poster board (see below). If desired, have the birthday child decorate each one individually. Suggest using glitter, feathers, scraps of lace, and fabric to create her own unique invitations. Write the invitation information on the back.

• Purchase a white handkerchief for each guest. Write the party information on the handkerchief with fabric markers.

Using construction paper, cut two handbags and glue three sides of the handbags together leaving the top portion of the handbags open. Insert the handkerchief into the handbag with a portion peeking out. Mail or hand deliver to your party guests.

DECORATIONS

1. Cut a large hat from poster board to cover the front door. Decorate it with sequins, glitter, lace, and fabric. Do not forget a large feather.

2. Make a stage to be used for the fashion show. (For instructions see Dance Party Decorations, page 23.) Use a white plastic tablecloth to make a runway leading to the stage.

3. Use construction paper to make shapes representing dress up accessories, such as hats, dresses, shoes and rings. Thread them onto seven foot lengths of string and hang them from the entrance doorway. The children will enjoy walking through them to enter the party.

4. Arrange the sashes, which will be given out at the **Award Ceremony** (see Games, page 64), on a decorated table in the party area.

REFRESHMENTS

Party Dress Cake: Bake your favorite cake mix in a 9" × 13" pan. Cut the cake as shown in the diagram (see right). Decorate the dress with candied stars or flowers. Use red licorice laces for the piping on the dress. Fill the heart with candy sprinkles.

Tea Sandwiches: Make open-face sandwiches by spreading cream cheese onto slices of party rye bread. Top each with a vegetable or fruit. Serve on a tray lined with paper doilies.

Fruit-Fun Dip:
    8 ounces cream cheese   ¼ cup sugar
    ¾ cup brown sugar   1 teaspoon vanilla

Combine the ingredients and refrigerate until chilled. Arrange a variety of fresh fruit on a platter and serve with the fruit dip.

Frozen Sparklers:
    1 pound frozen or fresh   32 ounces lemon-lime soda
      strawberries   (chilled)
    12-ounce can frozen lemonade
      concentrate (thawed)

Blend the strawberries in a blender until smooth. Stir in the lemonade concentrate. Freeze overnight in an airtight container. To serve, allow the strawberry mixture to soften slightly. Divide the mixture evenly into six glasses. Top with the soda. Stir slightly to make a slush. Garnish with a strawberry on the rim of the glass.

PARTY FAVORS

- Cut picture frames from poster board. The guests can decorate their frames with glitter. Take an instant photo of the guests and glue it in the picture frame.
- Make purses from metallic fabric and tie with drawstrings (see illustration A). You will need a 10" × 16" piece of fabric for each purse. Fold the fabric in half and stitch the sides together. Fold in the upper edge of the purse and stitch to form a casing. Insert the drawstring through the casing and knot the ends. Fill the purse with samples of perfume, tissues, mirrors, combs, or jewelry.
- Purchase an accordion fan for each guest. These can be used in the **Purse 'n' Hankie** game, see page 62.
- Cut pieces of wallpaper samples into 4" × 8" rectangles. Fold the rectangles into accordion fans (see illustration B). Fold up the bottom of the fans one inch and staple each fan to the back side of nut cups. Fill with candy.

A

B

CRAFTS

Fanciful Hats: (see illustration, page 60)

1 white gallon milk jug	2 24-inch pieces of 1-inch
1 12-inch white poster	wide ribbon
board circle	assorted ornamentation,
1 24-inch piece of 1½-inch	such as feathers,
wide ribbon	sequins, flowers, stickers

a) Cut the top off of the milk jug, leaving 3 inches at the bottom.
b) For the brim of the hat, cut a 5-inch circle from the center of the poster board, to fit a child's head.
c) Invert the milk jug and use a hot-melt glue gun to attach it to the center of the brim.
d) Punch two holes on opposite sides of the brim.

e) Let the children decorate their hats by gluing the 1½-inch wide ribbon around the hat and accenting with the assorted ornamentations.

f) Thread the 24-inch ribbons through each hole and knot above the brim (see above).

Marble Necklace:
2½" × 36" piece of fabric
6 marbles
7 beads

Fold the fabric, right sides together, and sew a seam along the two long sides, ⅛ inch from the edge. Turn the tube right side out. Tie a knot in one end about two to three inches from the edge.

Thread the open end of the tube through one bead and push the bead against the knot. Insert one marble into the tube and push it against the bead. Continue, alternating marbles and beads, until all beads and marbles are in place.

Tie a knot at the other end of the tube and tie both ends together to make the necklace (see below).

Heart Necklace:

1 wooden heart cutout waterbase paint
28-inch length of ribbon tiny pearl beads

Drill a hole on both sides of the heart. Paint the heart and, when dry, glue the pearl beads around the edge of the heart. A blow dryer will help dry the paint quickly.

Thread the ribbon through the two holes and then tie the ends together to make a necklace.

Braided Barrettes:

1 45-inch piece of ribbon 1 plain barrette with a
  (⅛ inch wide) slit in the middle
1 45-inch contrasting ribbon 2 small beads
  (⅛ inch wide) 1 colorful button

Tie the ends of the ribbons together to make one 90-inch piece. Lay the open end of the barrette on top of the knot. Insert one end of the ribbon through the slit and pull that color through. Pull the other end of the ribbon on the other side of the barrette until tight. Continue the weaving motion until the barrette is completely woven. Knot the ribbon at the end of the barrette. Tie the beads to the ends of the ribbon. Hot glue the button onto the barrette (see below).

GAMES

Rob Your Fancy Neighbor: Place three different colored handkerchiefs in a large purse. For each guest you will need approximately two to three small prizes. Wrap the prizes in colored wrapping papers to correspond with the colored handkerchiefs.

To begin the game, have everyone sitting in a circle. Place all the wrapped prizes in the center of the circle. Give the purse to the birthday child and have her pick out one handkerchief without peeking. She will then choose one prize wrapped in the matching colored paper. (No one opens any of the gifts until the game is over.) She will pass the purse to the next child and that child will do the same, and so forth.

When all the presents of a particular color are gone from the center of the circle and someone picks that color handkerchief, she will take a present, of that color, from one of her fancy neighbors.

The length of this game can vary. Be sure to give everyone a chance to rob a neighbor, and do not end the game until everyone has one or two gifts sitting in front of her. Conclude the game by letting everyone open her prizes.

What's Missing? The group should sit facing in one direction. Let the birthday child start the game by standing and facing her guests for approximately 15 seconds. The guests will be studying everything she is wearing.

The birthday child will leave the room and change one thing about her attire. She may decide to switch a ring to a different finger, or remove a necklace. She then returns to her guests and stands the exact same way. The guests will try to guess what she has changed. Continue the game until everyone has had a chance to change something about herself.

Purse 'n' Hankie: Give each guest one facial tissue and a fan. Divide the children into teams. The first child on each team will place her tissue on the floor and fan it into an opened purse lying on its side across the room. When she has successfully fanned the tissue into the purse, the next child on the team will begin. The first team to have all its hankies in the purse wins.

Pass the Jewels: Divide the group into teams. Each team will stand in a line. Place a gift box filled with jewels (marbles) at the beginning of each line. Place a jewelry box at the end of each line. Give each child one high-heeled shoe.

To begin the game, the first child on each team will pick up a jewel and place it in her shoe. She will then pass the jewel to the next child's shoe. As the jewel progresses down the line, the first child is continuously passing another jewel. The last child in line will place the jewels in the jewelry box. The first team to place all its jewels in the jewelry box wins the game.

Restaurant: Set up a play restaurant at the party and let the guests come in their fanciest clothes to "dine." Print menus for the party. Offer three or four selections of treats and list the prices. Give the children play money to use for payment.

Divide the guests into two groups. As the first half of the guests dine, the other half will be the waitresses. When the first group has finished eating, switch roles. Be sure to give the waitresses an apron, order pad, and pencil. Have large trays and pitchers on hand for serving the guests. If desired, use cloth napkins, tablecloths, china, crystal, and silver trays.

Sample menu:

WELCOME TO AMY'S CAFE

Tea Sandwiches	$2.00
Petit Fours	$1.00
Cupcake	$1.00
Nut Cups with Candy	$1.00
Frozen Sparklers	$2.00
After Dinner Mint	$1.00

Let's Have a Fashion Show! Prepare the "models" for the fashion show. Offer an assortment of additional dress up accessories. Do makeovers for those not wearing makeup. If time permits, paint their fingernails and fix their hair.

Make a stage for the fashion show (see Dance Party Decorations, page 73). Use a white plastic tablecloth for the runway. Mount a spotlight to shine on the models. Play or sing the theme song from the Miss America Pageant. An adult with a microphone can announce and describe each model as she crosses the stage.

Talent Show: After each model has been introduced in the fashion show, bring the group together for a talent show. We recommend this as a group activity due to the shyness of some of the guests.

Stand everyone on the runway. Sing the song below to the tune of "Old McDonald Had a Farm," using the birthday child's name.

For each verse insert a different guest's name. At that time, the guest will take one step forward and make a motion which everyone will follow, such as clapping hands, swaying to-and-fro, stomping feet, etc. After each verse is sung, that guest will return to her place in line and the next child will have a turn.

Susie Kramer had a birthday,
La, la, la, la, la.
At her party there was Katie,
La, la, la, la, la.
With a Katie, Katie here,
And a Katie, Katie there,

Here a Katie,
There a Katie,
Everywhere a Katie, Katie.
Susie Kramer had a birthday,
La, la, la, la, la.

Award Ceremony: Award sashes to each child in the show. Use 4-inch wide ribbon and write the title of the award across the front. Announce all the winners and have them come to the center of the stage for their sash.

Suggested awards:

The Prettiest	The Friendliest
The Most Beautiful	The Best Singer
The Most Colorful	Miss 1995
The Fanciest	Miss America

Flower Party

INVITATIONS

- Make a daisy using yellow and green construction paper. On the petals write the necessary information for the party.
- Make a pop up invitation using a piece of construction paper. Fold the bottom edge 1½" from the top edge (see A). Fold in half, with the tall side in (see B). Draw petals on the fold. Cut away the remaining paper (see C). Open the card flat, keeping the short side behind. Draw the flower (see D). Bring down the right corner and crease from the end of the petal to the center fold (see E). Repeat with the opposite corner (see F). Fold top, center line of petal in and close card (see G). Decorate as desired. On the front of the invitation write "There's a Party Blooming at My House!" (see H). Write the party information on the inside of the invitation.

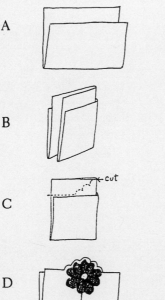

DECORATIONS

1. Hang large tissue flowers in the party area. Make one for each child to take home as a party favor.

Center one 16″ × 26″ sheet of tissue paper on top of three 20″ × 26″ sheets of contrasting tissue paper. Fanfold all the sheets of paper together into folds of approximately one inch. Tie the center tight with a twist tie or wire. Carefully pull each layer of the paper towards the center.

2. Make flower candy holders (see illustration A) for the party guests and place them at the party table. Open a dinner napkin and lay it flat. Fold the four corners to meet at the center of the napkin. Fold the four new corners to the center again, and repeat a third time. Turn the napkin over and fold these four corners to the center. Turn the napkin to the original side and place over a cup. Pull the first four corners down over the cup. Do the same for the second layer and the third. Lift the candy holder off the cup. Fill the holder with candy treats.

A   B

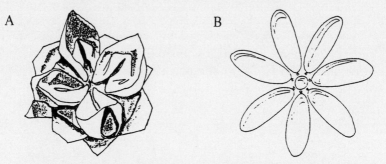

3. Place balloons in a flower pattern on the wall (see illustration B). Use a small round balloon in the center and oblong balloons as the petals.

4. Tape large cutout flowers to the back of each guest's chair.

5. Use vases with fresh flowers to accent the party area.

REFRESHMENTS

Wheelbarrow Cupcakes: Make your favorite cupcake recipe and frost cupcakes in desired colored frosting. Insert two 3-inch pipe cleaners into the cupcake for the wheelbarrow handles (see right). String one ring-shaped piece of hard candy onto a 4-inch piece of pipe cleaner and insert into the cupcake for the wheel.

Edible Flowers:

12 vanilla wafers   24 green spearmint leaves
12 strings red licorice   frosting
12 bubble gum sticks

This is a refreshment the children will enjoy preparing for themselves. Place a vanilla wafer in the center of a paper plate. Frost the wafer and place loops of red licorice on the wafer to form petals. Place a bubble gum stick at the bottom of the wafer for a stem and set the spearmint leaves along the bubble gum (see below). Makes 12 flowers.

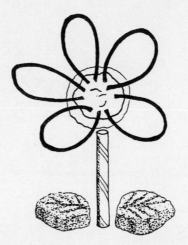

Flower Cookies:

1 20-ounce roll of refrigerated   new, clean paintbrushes
   cookie dough   1 egg yolk
30 craft sticks   ¼ teaspoon water
food coloring

Place the sticks on an ungreased cookie sheet. Slice ¼-inch slices of cookie dough and place the dough slices onto the stick. The cookies should be at least three inches apart. Press each slice of dough with your fingers to about three inches in diameter.

Mix the egg yolk and water and divide into two small bowls. Add three drops of food coloring to each bowl. Stir well. Paint the dough with the egg yolk mixture to resemble flowers.

Bake at 350 degrees for 7 to 11 minutes (until golden brown). Cool the cookies on the cookie sheet for one minute, and then cool them on a wire rack.

Glue green construction paper leaves onto the wooden sticks.

Makes about 30 flower cookies.

Flower Pots: Layer the following into a small paper cup (see right):
  1 scoop of chocolate ice cream or pudding
  crushed chocolate cookies for "dirt"
  1 red plastic spoon (centered in the ice cream to
    represent a red tulip)
  2 spearmint leaves placed into the dirt at the
    base of the spoon
  insert gummy worms coming out of the dirt
    hanging over the edge of the "flower pot"

Daisy-Burgers: Grill one hamburger for each child. Draw a flower with ketchup on top of the burger. Place a pickle in the center of the flower. Serve open-faced with french fries on the side.

PARTY FAVORS

- Purchase sprinkling cans for each guest and fill with party favors.
- Vases or flower pots can be painted and used as a container for party favors.

Suggested favors: plastic garden tools, seed packages, garden gloves, artificial flowers, gummy worms, sunflower seeds, potted plants.

CRAFTS

Place Mats and Coasters: Cut out pictures of flowers from old greeting cards, magazines, or wallpaper. Cut an 18-inch length of Contact paper with a flower design. Arrange the pictures on the sticky side of the Contact paper. Cover the place mat with clear Contact paper and trim to even the edges.

Make a smaller coaster as described above to match the place mat. Let the guests use these at the refreshment table.

Decorated Flower Pots: Cover an empty can with wallpaper and glue the wallpaper in place. Fill the pot with potting soil and have the guests plant seeds or small bedding plants.

Corsages:

2½" × 2½" square of poster board	12-inch contrasting satin ribbon, ¼ inch wide
½-inch craft pin	1 small decorative flower
24-inch satin ribbon, ¼ inch wide	1-inch bar pin

Place the craft pin in the center of the poster board square. Place the poster board on a flat surface so that the pin point is sticking up.

Take the end of the 24-inch ribbon and place it on the pin. Make a loop the length of the poster board and stick the ribbon onto the pin. Continue making ribbon loops until you have used the length of the ribbon (approximately seven loops). Attach the 12-inch ribbon to the pin on top of the ribbon you have just completed, making smaller loops. Continue to the end of the ribbon (approximately six loops) (see below).

Using a hot-melt glue gun, attach the decorative flower in the center of the corsage. Snip the point off of the craft pin.

Trim the poster board so it does not show, leaving enough room for the bar pin. Hot glue the bar pin to the back of the corsage.

Flower Child: Cut out the center of a 9-inch paper plate and discard. Cut petals from colored construction paper and glue around the outer edge of the plate. Staple the ends of an 18-inch piece of elastic to both sides of the plate so the party guests can wear it as a mask.

Make a badge for the "flower children" to wear. Write on the badge the instructions for "How to Care for Me" and cover it with clear Contact paper. Attach with a safety pin to the "Flower Child."

How to Care for Me:

Plant type: Perennial
Light: Most active during daylight hours. When dark, tuck me into bed with a story, hug and kiss.
Water: Keep moist with plenty of water and juice. Occasional bathing is necessary.

Temperature: Maintain at 98.6 degrees

Fertilize: I need three meals a day for a strong healthy plant. Snacks will provide extra foliage. Be sure to nourish with daily affection.

Note: Research indicates plants thrive when talked to. Please tell me you love me every day!

Fabric Flowers:

assorted colored fabrics (small calico prints preferred)

pom-pom

contrasting colored pipe cleaners

floral tape

a) Cut the fabrics into petals (five petals per flower).

b) Starting at the base of the petal, glue a pipe cleaner around the edge. Twist the end of the pipe cleaner to the beginning part of the pipe cleaner at the base.

c) Using floral tape, wrap the petal bases together and attach them to a pipe cleaner stem.

d) Glue the pom-pom to the center (see below).

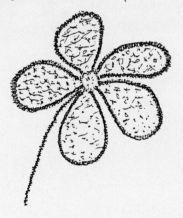

Painted Flower Pots: Purchase a potted flower for each guest. Wipe the pots to make sure the surface area is clean. Paint designs on the flower pots using acrylic, waterbase paint.

GAMES

"I'm a Flower" Relay: For each team you will need approximately twelve clothespins. Using construction paper, design leaves, petals, butterflies, worms, ladybugs, raindrops and flower pots, and glue each of them to a clothespin.

Divide the party guests into teams. Have one flower pot for each team, containing the assortment of flower parts. Set the flower pot about 15 feet away from the teams.

The first person on each team will run to the flower pot and attach all the clothespins onto her clothing to make her look like a flower. She will then run back to the second child in line and tag her. When the second child has been tagged, the first runner removes all the clothespins and the second child will attach them to herself. She then runs to the flower pot and back, tags the third player, and transfers the clothespins to her, and so on. The last player on the team will run to the flower pot, remove the clothespins, deposit them into the pot, and run back to the first child in line and tag her. The first team to have all its clothespins in the flower pot is the winner.

Beautiful Bouquets: Each child must find one each of assorted silk or plastic flowers that have been hidden throughout the party area. No one may find the same flower twice.

After all the flowers have been found, give each child a small vase or flower pot. Place a small piece of Styrofoam inside the vase. Let the children arrange the flowers in their vase and take home as a party favor.

Water the Flower Relay: For each team you will need the following items:

1 large vase containing an artificial flower	1 small sprinkling can
	1 large bucket filled with water

Divide the group into teams. Place the bucket of water and the sprinkling can by each team. Place the vase with the flower at the opposite end of the party area, about 15 feet away.

Each child must dip the sprinkling can into the bucket of water, run to the vase to water the flower, run back to her team and hand the sprinkling can to the next runner. She will then fill the can and run to water the flower. The first team that fills its vase to the top is the winner.

Garden Glove Relay: Divide the guests into teams. Each team will need one bag containing one pair of garden gloves and a piece of wrapped candy for each team member.

Each team will sit in a row. The first child on each team will put on the garden gloves, remove a piece of candy from the bag, unwrap and eat the candy. She then removes the gloves, places them back in the bag, and passes the bag to her teammate. Continue down the row. The first team to finish is the winner.

Do What I Do! Make flower petals from construction paper. On each petal write a different direction for an activity. Using toothpicks, insert the flower petals into a Styrofoam ball. Mount the ball on a pencil and insert the pencil in a flower pot filled with dirt.

Give each child a turn to remove a petal from the "flower" and be the leader of the activity. Repeat each action, in order, adding on each new activity as another child picks a petal.

Suggestions:

a) hop like a bunny in a garden
b) sway to-and-fro like flowers on a windy day
c) buzz like a bumblebee
d) pretend to be a seed and grow into a tall flower
e) droop like a flower needing water
f) be a ladybug and crawl through the garden

Name the Flower: On separate sheets of construction paper, glue pictures of flowers. Label each picture with the name of the flower. Display these pictures around the party area, placing some in less obvious locations.

Print a worksheet with a description of each flower's name followed by a blank line.

The guests will search for all the pictures and fill in the blanks with the correct flower name. The person who has correctly named the most flowers in the allotted time is the winner. Sample worksheet:

NAME THE FLOWER

a) You can kiss with these. (tulips)
b) A young Girl Scout is called this. (daisy)
c) A dozen of these are given on Valentine's Day. (roses)
d) This is Porky Pig's girlfriend. (petunia)
e) A name you might call your mother. (mum)
f) The name of a girl who has yellow hair. (marigold)
g) A brand of instant breakfast drink. (carnation)
h) This name will remind you of Daffy Duck. (daffodil)
i) An infant's intake of air. (baby's breath)
j) Roses are red and these are blue. (violets)
k) You will find this flower "Down in the _____ where the green grass grows." (lily of the valley)
l) Pull out the stem for a sweet surprise. Also, bees like to make this sweet surprise. (honeysuckle)
m) A feeling when you can not wait for something to happen. (impatiens)

Dance Party

INVITATIONS

• Make a musical invitation on a cassette and mail one to each guest. Below is an example of a rap song which you could use:

Now is the time to get together,
So come on down and let's party forever.
Julie's house is the place to be,
There's going to be dance fever from one o'clock to three.
Don't be afraid to come out in any weather,
January 3rd is when we're gettin' together.
We need to know by next week if you'll attend,
It just wouldn't be the same without my friend!

• Cut out a circle the size of a record from construction paper. Punch a hole in the middle of the circle and attach a label to the center. Write the necessary invitation information around the record.

DECORATIONS

1. Make a small stage for the dancers. The stage is made with two-by-fours and a sheet of ½-inch plywood. Lay the boards on their sides at right angles, forming a rectangle. Nail the plywood to the top.
2. Mount a spotlight to shine on the stage.
3. Decorate the walls with record albums and a jukebox cut from construction paper.
4. Hang a mirrored glass ball from the ceiling.
5. Use strobe lights to liven the atmosphere when the guests are dancing.
6. Cut pictures of dancers from magazines to decorate the party area.

7. Make a cardboard jukebox to cover your stereo cabinet (see illustration A).

8. A centerpiece can be made by gluing a glass Coke bottle to the center of a 45 rpm record. Partially fill the bottle with brown sand. Insert two straws into the bottle (see illustration B).

A   B

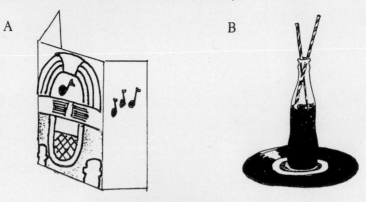

REFRESHMENTS

Happy Birthday Record Cake: Bake your favorite cake mix in two 9-inch round pans. After the cake has cooled, frost with chocolate frosting. Using a toothpick, draw grooves in the frosting in a circular pattern to resemble the grooves on a record. Prepare a record label from poster board and write "Happy Birthday Julie" on it. Center the label on top of the cake.

Fruit Smoothie:
4 ripe bananas   2 cups strawberries,
1 pint lemon sherbet   cut in half

Combine the ingredients in a blender. Blend until smooth and pour into fluted glasses. Garnish with a strawberry on the rim of the glass. Makes four servings.

Mini-Cheesecakes:
12 vanilla wafers   1 teaspoon vanilla
2 8-ounce packages   2 eggs
    cream cheese   Toppings: fruit, preserves,
½ cup sugar   or shaved chocolate

Line a muffin tin with foil liners. Place one vanilla wafer in each liner. Mix cream cheese, vanilla, and sugar until well blended. Add eggs.

Mix well. Pour mixture over the wafers, filling ¾ full. Bake 25 minutes at 325 degrees. Remove from pan when cool. Chill. Add desired topping. Makes 12 cheesecakes.

Big Heart Dancers:
Chocoate Dancers:

¼ cup margarine	⅓ cup semisweet chocolate
10-ounce package miniature	chips
marshmallows	6 cups crisp rice cereal

Red Dancers:

¼ cup margarine	2 to 3 drops red food coloring
10-ounce package miniature	6 cups crisp rice cereal
marshmallows	

To make the chocolate dancers (see below), line a 15″ × 10″ × 1″ jelly roll pan with aluminum foil. Melt the margarine over low heat in a large saucepan. Add the marshmallows and chocolate, stirring until completely melted. Remove from heat and add the cereal. Stir until well coated. Using a buttered spatula or fingers, press into the pan. Let cool and remove the mixture from the pan by lifting the foil.

To make the red dancers, repeat the directions above, substituting the red food coloring for the chocolate chips.

Using a 5-inch gingerbread man cookie cutter, cut eight dancers from each pan. With a 1-inch heart-shaped cookie cutter, cut hearts from the center of each dancer. Exchange the hearts between the dancers so the chocolate dancer will have a red heart and the red dancer will have a chocolate heart.

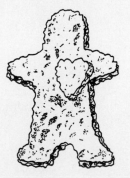

Dancers Delight: Slice dollar rolls in half and serve with a variety of fillings, such as chicken salad, tuna salad, luncheon meats, or cheese.

PARTY FAVORS

- For uniformity when dancing, give each dancer matching hats, socks, gloves, or belts.
- Fill a small gift bag with earrings, necklaces, pins, candy and stickers.
- Include with your thank-you notes a copy of the video you made of the dances.

CRAFTS

Fancy Dancin'! Decorate hats, gloves, or socks with fabric markers for the guests to wear while dancing.

Glitter Stars: Cut a star from poster board for each guest. When the guests arrive, have them make up a stage name for themselves and write it on the star. Let the dancers decorate their star with glue and glitter and have them wear it during the party. Call them by their stage name.

Ballet Slipper Potpourri: Cut two pieces of felt in the shape of a ballet slipper. Sew around the edges leaving an opening at the top. Stuff with potpourri and finish sewing it closed.

Use tacky glue to attach dried flowers, ribbons, sequins, or stars. Attach a loop, made with ribbon, to the back of the slipper for hanging.

GAMES

Follow the Music: Collect a variety of music. Play each type of music for one to two minutes. The dancers must dance a style appropriate to the sound and feel of the music.

Examples: Rock 'n' Roll, Ballroom, Oriental, Jazz, Rap, Country and Western, Opera, Gospel, Hawaiian, Indian, Drum Instrumental.

One-Man Dance Show: Put the **Glitter Star** name tags (see Crafts above) into a top hat. Play the music and have everyone dance. Stop the music intermittently. Pick a star's name from the hat, and have that dancer go to the stage and put on a "One-Man Dance Show" for about one minute. Continue until every dancer has had a chance to perform.

Dance Contest: Video tape the **Follow the Music** or the **One-Man Dance Show** (see page 76). Replay the tape and let the guests judge the dancers. Give out awards for the Silliest Dancer, Most Original Dancer, Best Hawaiian Dancer, and Best Rock 'n' Roll Dancer. Be sure to have one award for every child at the party.

Dance Performance: Teach the dancers a simple dance routine to practice at the party or have each one of the guests make up her own dance step for everyone to follow and incorporate them into a routine. Perform the dance the girls have learned for their parents at the conclusion of the party.

Examples: a Square Dance, the Mexican Hat Dance, the Hokey Pokey, the Bump, the Monkey, the Swim, the Twist, the Pony, the Worm, the Moonwalk, the Jitterbug, the Locomotion, the Limbo, the Hula, or the Charleston.

Sock Hop: Make one "poodle" skirt for each girl (see below). For each skirt, cut a felt circle 50 inches in diameter or seam together two semicircles. Cut a circle 12 inches in diameter from the center of the fabric for the waist. Fold the waist over one inch and stitch to make a casing for the elastic waistband. Insert elastic through the casing to fit a child's waist.

At the party have the guests draw poodles on their skirts with fabric markers or make felt poodle cutouts and attach with tacky glue to the skirts.

Focus your music on the 50s and 60s rock 'n' roll songs. Play an "oldie" and let the children dance to it. Have them rate the record. Score the songs from one to ten. Ask them if it had a good beat and if it was easy to dance to.

Serve shakes or ice cream sodas from your "malt shop" for refreshments.

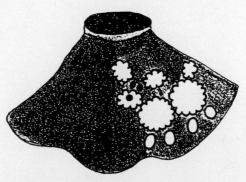

Stroll on Down: Divide the guests into pairs and have the pairs form two lines (six feet apart) with the partners facing each other. Start the music and have the partners at the beginning of the lines dance between the two lines. When they are finished, they go to the end of their original line, facing each other again, and the next couple strolls on down.

The guests who are standing in line are dancing in place to the beat of the music. Continue the song until everyone has had a turn to stroll.

Beat to the Music: For each person you will need two Lummi sticks. Lummi sticks can be made by cutting a 1-inch wooden dowel rod into 15-inch lengths.

Divide the children into pairs. Have them sit Indian style facing their partner. Play music with a distinct beat and have the children tap their sticks on the floor and against their partner's sticks (right to right, left to left) to the consistent rhythm.

Half the group can play their sticks while the others dance to the beat. After a few minutes, switch the groups and have the players become the dancers and vice versa.

Slumber Party

INVITATIONS

• Cut two sleeping bags from construction paper. Glue around the edges, leaving the top open. Using a contrasting color, cut a paper doll. Write the invitation information on the paper doll and insert it into the sleeping bag.

• Glue a 9″ × 6″ piece of black construction paper onto a 9″ × 6″ piece of blue construction paper. Fold in half, with the black on the outside and the blue on the inside. Cover the outside with a moon and stars (see below). Cut a 3½-inch sun from yellow construction paper. Glue the sun to the inside of the invitation. Write the party information on the sun. In the blue "sky" write, "It would be a delight if you'd come party overnight!"

DECORATIONS

1. Set up a **Beauty Salon** (see Games page 82) in the party area. Include in the salon rollers, makeup, nail polish, and accessories to change the guests from ordinary children into raving beauties.

2. Hang a mirrored ball from the ceiling. When it is time for "lights out," shine a flashlight on the ball and watch the show.

3. Hang cutouts in the shape of records, telephones, pillows, and sleeping bags from the ceiling and on the walls.

4. Decorate with posters of the latest music and movie stars or other teen idols.

REFRESHMENTS

Giant Chocolate Chip Cookie: Beat until creamy:

1 cup butter	¾ cup brown sugar
¾ cup sugar	1 teaspoon vanilla extract

Beat in 2 eggs. Gradually add in a mixture of:

2¼ cups flour	1 teaspoon salt
1 teaspoon baking soda	

Stir in 2 cups semisweet chocolate chips.

Spread into a greased 15" × 10" × 1" baking pan. Bake in a preheated 375 degree oven for 20 to 25 minutes. Cool. Use decorator frosting to write a happy birthday message across the giant cookie. Cut into 2-inch squares to serve.

Ice Cream Bar: Give each child one scoop of vanilla ice cream. Offer an assortment of toppings, such as chocolate syrup, marshmallow cream, sliced bananas, strawberries, nuts, mini chocolate chips, candy sprinkles, whipped cream and a cherry for the top.

Pita Pocket Pizzas:

1 pound Italian sausage (browned and drained)	15 ounce jar spaghetti sauce
½ pound pepperoni, coursely chopped	2 cups shredded mozzarella cheese
	6 pita pockets, cut in half

In a large bowl, combine sausage, pepperoni, sauce and one cup of cheese. Divide the meat mixture evenly into the pita pocket halves. Divide the remaining cheese among the pita pockets. Place on a baking sheet. Bake at 350 degrees, 15 to 20 minutes or until cheese melts. Makes 12 pizzas.

Variation: If the children are cooking their own snacks, give them each a pita pocket. Spoon into the pockets one tablespoon of sauce, one tablespoon of cheese and one or two of their favorite pizza toppings. Bake as directed above.

Breakfast Tarts: Give each child one refrigerated biscuit. Press flat on a greased baking pan. Sprinkle with sugar and cinnamon. Put one tablespoon of pie filling in the center of the biscuit. Fold over to form a semicircle and press the edges together. Bake for 8 minutes at 475 degrees.

Shish Kebab for Breakfast: Cut apples, pineapple, cantaloupe, cooked sausage links, cooked ham, and English muffins and place into separate bowls. Give each child a skewer and let the children create their own shish kebab.

PARTY FAVORS

• Purchase quilted fabric to make small sleeping bags to hold the favors (see right). For each sleeping bag, cut an 11″ × 12″ piece of the fabric. Fold the 12-inch length in half, right sides together, and stitch the side and bottom together with a ¼-inch seam. Turn right side out and finish off the top edge. Fill with treats. When empty, the sleeping bag can be used for the guests' 11-inch dolls.

• Purchase cosmetic bags or make the **Painted Pillowcases** (see Crafts below) as goody bags.

• *Suggested favors:* jewelry, nail polish, makeup, hair accessories, soap, bubble bath, personalized toothbrushes, teen magazines, paper dolls.

CRAFTS

"My Dream Life" Scrapbook: For each child, place ten pieces of construction paper inside a folder with brads. Label the top of each page as listed below. Offer an assortment of magazines. (Bridal and family magazines are ideal.) The guests will cut out magazine pictures and glue them into their books to show their future dreams.

    page 1: The Boy of My Dreams
    page 2: My Prom Dress
    page 3: My Wedding Dress
    page 4: My Flower Girl's Dress
    page 5: My Occupation
    page 6: My House
    page 7: My Car
    page 8: My Vacation
    page 9: My Beautiful Garden
    page 10: My Babies

Painted Pillowcases: Purchase one white pillowcase for each guest. Decorate the pillowcases with fabric paints or fabric markers. Paints will need to dry overnight.

Loop Barrettes: From your local craft store, purchase plain hair barrettes and jersey weaving loops. Remove the center bar from the barrette and set it aside.

Tie the loops into double knots around the barrette until it is completely covered (see below). Insert the center bar into each barrette. Use the barrettes when styling the guests' hair in the **Beauty Salon** (see Games below).

GAMES

Beauty Salon: Let the girls practice their cosmetic skills in the "Beauty Salon." Include everything they need for giving each other facials, applying makeup, and doing manicures and pedicures. Style the guests' hair using curling irons, electric rollers, and crimpers. If you made the **Loop Barrettes** (see Crafts above), incorporate them into the hair style.

Scavenger Hunt: Divide the guests into small groups. Give each group a list of objects to find. Depending on the ages of the children, you can have a scavenger hunt within the party area or a house-to-house hunt (with adult supervision for each group). The first group to find everything on its list and make it back to "base" is the winner.

Roller Relay: Divide the guests into teams and have each team stand in a line. The first child on each team will sit in a chair approximately ten feet away from her teammates. Place a container of sponge curlers next to each chair.

To begin the relay, the first child in line runs up to the child in the chair and puts one roller in her hair. The child with the roller in her hair runs to the end of the line and the first runner sits in the chair. Repeat with each child running up, putting in a curler, sitting in the chair to get a curler, and then running to the end of the line. The game continues until each child on the team has five rollers in her hair. The first team completely "rolled" is the winner.

Sleeping Bag Roll Over: Lay all the sleeping bags side by side in one long line. Stand the guests in a line at the first bag. Sing the song "Ten in a Bed." When the words "roll over" are sung, the first child will begin doing log rolls across the sleeping bags. Once the child is on the third sleeping bag, have the second child start rolling across the bags. Continue singing the song until everyone has rolled over all the sleeping bags.

"Ten in a Bed"
There were ten in a bed,
and the little one said,
"Roll over, roll over."
So they all rolled over and one fell out.
There were nine in the bed,
and the little one said,
"Roll over, roll over."
So they all rolled over and one fell out.
(Continue the song until you get to "one")
There was one in the bed,
and the little one said,
"Good night!"

Did You Hear? For each child at the party, prepare a sheet of paper containing a short phrase. All the guests will sit in a circle. The first child will pick a piece of paper and read it to herself. She will mentally complete the phrase and then whisper it to the child on her right. That child whispers it to the child on her right. This passing of the phrase continues until the phrase has gone completely around the circle.

When the last girl has heard the phrase, have her say it out loud. The play continues until everyone has had a turn to start a phrase. Suggest that once a name is used, it cannot be repeated.

Suggestions for phrases:

a) Did you hear that _____ would like to marry _____?
b) Did you hear that _____ wants _____ to kiss her?
c) Did you hear that (Teacher's name) thinks _____ is funny?
d) Did you hear that _____ thinks _____ reminds her of a monkey?
e) Did you hear that if _____ was an animal he would be a _____?
f) Did you hear that when _____ gets married she wants to have 18 children?
g) Did you hear that _____ wishes she could go on a date with _____?
h) Did you hear that _____ would like to be a clown in the circus?

PJs in the Bag: Each guest will lay out her sleeping bag and put her pajamas inside the bag. When you signal to begin the game, the guests will get inside of their sleeping bags and change from their clothes into their PJs. The first child to put on her pajamas while remaining inside the sleeping bag is the winner.

Bedtime Story: As the guests are lying in their sleeping bags, turn out the lights and shine flashlights on a mirrored ball. Tell them a story and then say "Good night."

Dinosaur Party

INVITATIONS

- From colored construction paper, cut an egg and a dinosaur shape (see below). Cut a "crack" line across the center of the egg. Glue the bottom of the dinosaur to the bottom part of the egg. Insert a brad through both the top and bottom portions of the egg. Write the necessary party information on the dinosaur.

- Fold a piece of green construction paper in half and cut a dinosaur shape. Cut out the mouth from the top part of the invitation. Write the word "roaring," so that the "roar" part of the word can be seen through the dinosaur's mouth. Write on the inside, "Come to my dinosaur party for a roaring good time."

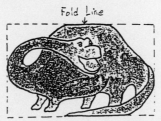

Fold Line

DECORATIONS

1. Place dinosaur footprints on the walkway leading to the party area.

2. Tape a large poster or cutout of a dinosaur on the front door.

3. Make a wall mural with pictures your child has colored of various dinosaurs.

4. Purchase a white paper tablecloth. Sponge print dinosaur designs onto the tablecloth by dipping dinosaur sponges into waterbase paints and applying to the tablecloth.

5. Purchase balloons with dinosaurs on them. Hang them from the ceiling and accent with crepe paper streamers.

REFRESHMENTS

Dinosaur Cake: Bake your favorite cake mix in a 9″×13″ pan. Trace a dinosaur pattern onto waxed paper and place the pattern on the cake. Cut the cake along the dotted lines. Frost and outline the dinosaur cake. Decorate with jelly beans for eyes, candy corn for teeth, red licorice for a smile, and marshmallows or round candy for spots (see below).

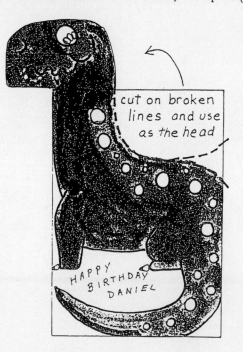

Art to Eat! This snack can also be the party craft.
creamy peanut butter
powdered milk
honey

Mix equal amounts of peanut butter and powdered milk. Add the honey until it is the consistency of clay. Divide it among the children and let them mold it into a dinosaur shape. When finished, let them eat their dinosaur!

Dino-Wiches:

12 slices of bread	6 slices of luncheon meat
6 slices of cheese	dinosaur cookie cutter

With the cookie cutter, cut out dinosaur shapes from the bread, cheese and luncheon meat. Assemble into six "Dino-Wiches." Serve "Dino-aid" as the drink.

Wiggling Dinosaurs:

4 6-ounce packages flavored gelatin
5 cups boiling water

Add boiling water to the gelatin and stir until gelatin is dissolved. Pour into a 10″ × 15″ pan. Chill until set. Use a cookie cutter to cut into dinosaur shapes. Eat with fingers.

PARTY FAVORS

• Decorate paper lunch bags with dinosaur shapes. Trace dinosaur stencils and color, decorate with stickers, or sponge paint designs (see **Dinosaur Sponge Prints** page 88).
• Use large, plastic eggs as dinosaur eggs and fill them with the party goodies.
• *Suggested favors:* dinosaur fruit snacks, plastic dinosaur toys, dinosaur stickers, dinosaur coloring books, crayons, candy.

CRAFTS

Dinosaur Prints: Pour plaster of paris (made according to directions on package) into small pie tins. Each child will press his hand print into the plaster of paris to make his own "fossil" print. When the fossils are dry, remove them from their pans and write each child's name on the bottom. Mix them up on a table and let the children try to find their own fossil print. If desired, paint the dry fossils with watercolor paints.

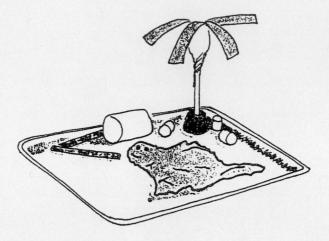

Dinosaur Land: Give each child a plastic plate or foam tray as the base for his "land" (see above). The children can make trees from lollipops stuck into gum drops, rocks from marshmallows, logs from pretzel sticks, etc. Give them frosting to use as "glue" for their land. Use the **Art to Eat** recipe (see Refreshments, page 87) to make the dough for the dinosaurs.

Dinosaur Sponge Prints: Begin the party with this craft to allow time for the paint to dry.

Give each child a white paper lunch bag and sponges cut into dinosaur shapes (available at your local craft store). Instruct the children to press the sponges into acrylic, waterbase paint and then onto their bags. Give them a choice of colors and sponges.

When the paint is dry, use these bags to carry the goodies in the **Cave Hunt** game (see page 90).

"Spike" the Stegosaurus: Cut a tissue roll as shown below. Draw the scales and eyes onto the tube. From poster board, cut out dinosaur legs and spikes and glue them into place.

To use this craft as a party favor, cover each end with a circle of poster board, fill with candy, and tape closed.

push to
fold nose
in

cut both
sides for
mouth

GAMES

Caveman and Hunter: From your local fabric store, purchase fake fur (or flannel printed like animal skin) to make caveman vests for each child. Cut armholes 8 inches in diameter and a neckline in a 24″ × 32″ piece of the fabric (see illustration A). Finish off the raw edges to avoid raveling.

Drape the animal skin (vest) over a small box (see illustration B). Make an animal face on a smaller box and place it on top of the skin. Make a tail from the fabric and place one end under the skin.

Tell the "cavemen" they must hunt animals and get skins to wear for warmth in the cold caves. Give the children large hoops and have them toss them trying to ring an animal. When the children succeed, they will remove the skin and wear their animal vests. Now they are ready to enter the cave to hunt for their artifacts.

A

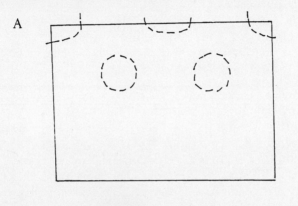

B

Hot-O-Saurus: Everyone will sit in a circle. As music is playing, pass a dinosaur toy around the circle. Stop the music intermittently and the child who is holding the dinosaur toy leaves the circle and will get in line for the **Cave Hunt** game (see page 90). Continue the game and the last remaining child is the winner.

Cave Hunt: Cover a table with a large blanket that touches the floor on all sides of the table. This is your "cave." Be sure it is dark inside. Pin dinosaur artifacts to the walls and fill the floor of the cave with dinosaur stickers, sponges, candy bones, and fruit snacks.

Each child will enter the cave alone with a flashlight and a goody bag. The goal of their hunt is to come out of the cave with one of each type of item hidden inside.

Since this is an individual activity, you should involve the other children in a group activity, such as the **Dinosaur Jingle** (see below), while each child is hunting.

Dinosaur Jingle: Sing this song to the tune of "If You're Happy and You Know It."

   a) Triceratops (tri-serr-a-tops) had three horns on their head.
      Triceratops had three horns on their head.
      That was long, long ago,
      And we really do miss them so.
      Triceratops had three horns on their head.
   b) Protoceratops (pro-tow-serr-ah-tops) had a beak like a bird...
   c) Compsognathus (comp-sog-nay-thus) was a little bitty guy...
   d) A Brontosaurus (bron-tow-saw-rus) was over 80 feet long...
   e) Stegosaurus (steg-oh-saw-rus) moved low on the ground...
   f) A Trachodon (track-oh-don) swam like a duck...
   g) Tyrannosaurus Rex (tie-ran-oh-saw-rus Rex) had big, sharp teeth...

Dinosaur Egg Hunt: Fill large plastic eggs with small dinosaur toys, candy, and stickers. Hide five eggs per child throughout the party area. After each child has found his five eggs, allow him time to open the eggs and see what he has found.

Feeding Time for the Dinosaurs: Hang dinosaur "food" on strings from trees or from the ceiling. The food can be cookies with a center hole, donuts, or pretzels. Each child will act like a Tyrannosaurus Rex. The children should hold their arms close to their sides, bend their elbows up and flex their wrists. On the count of three, they will "stomp" their way over to the trees. The children must eat their food without using their hands. The first "dinosaur" to finish is the winner.

Name the Mystery-Saur: Give each child the name of a dinosaur that he will be throughout the game. Everyone will sit in a line facing the "Tyrannosaurus Rex." Begin with the birthday child as the Tyrannosaurus Rex and have him sit on a "rock" (a small chair or carpet square) with his back to the other dinosaurs. Tyrannosaurus Rex must close his eyes and not peek. Tap one dinosaur on the back and that child will roar like a dinosaur. Tyrannosaurus Rex will try to guess which dinosaur made the sound. Give him one or two tries. The child that roared will be the next dinosaur on the rock. The game continues until everyone has had a turn on the rock.

For a more challenging game, suggest that the dinosaurs disguise their voices and change their positions.

Dinosaurs Go Home! Each child will need one straw and one piece of tissue paper cut into the shape of a dinosaur. Have the children practice holding the tissue paper dinosaur to the bottom of the straw by inhaling through the straw.

Divide the group into teams. The first person on each team inhales through the straw and carries his dinosaur, as fast as he can, across the party area to be put into its home, which is a box decorated like a forest. The child runs back and tags the second player on his team, and so on. The first team to get all its dinosaurs home, wins.

Hidden Egg Message: Prepare a scoreboard for each team on a sheet of poster board. On each scoreboard draw a path with ten spaces leading to a tree. Cut one dinosaur shape, from construction paper for each scoreboard.

You will need approximately thirty plastic eggs with a message inside of each egg. Write the messages on colored construction paper cut into the shape of a dinosaur. Use the following messages:

10 eggs—"Move ahead 1 space"
10 eggs—"Move ahead 2 spaces"
 6 eggs—"Move back 1 space"
 4 eggs—"Move back 2 spaces"

Prior to the party, hide all the eggs around the area. Divide the group into teams. The first player on each team runs to find an egg and brings it back to the team. He will read the message and move the dinosaur on his scoreboard accordingly. The second player will do the same and so on. Continue playing until a team moves its dinosaur to its tree to win.

Train Party

INVITATIONS

• Design a 3″ × 5″ index card to resemble a ticket for a train ride (see below). Be sure to indicate on the invitation to bring the ticket to the party. It will be used for an admission ticket.

All Aboard
Destination : Eric's Birthday Party
22 Oak St.
Time : 1:30 p.m - 3:30 p.m.
Date : Sat. June 1
R.S.V.P. : 123-4567

• Fold a 9″ × 12″ sheet of construction paper, as shown below. Draw train tracks across the outside of the invitation and write the words "You're on track to . . ." or "Follow the rails to . . ." Open to the inside and write "Eric's Birthday Party." Draw a train on your railroad tracks. Include party information on the inside of the invitation.

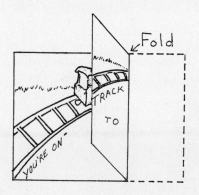

DECORATIONS

1. Cut a door in the back of a large, appliance-sized box to use as the entrance to the "depot." Cut a window in the front of the depot. Hang a sign at the top of the depot stating the name of the railway, such as "Eric's Express," and a chart of destinations and ticket prices.

At the beginning of the party, have the birthday child be the "Station Master." As he stands inside the depot he can take the tickets from his guests and welcome them to the party. Keep extra tickets available for guests who forget to bring them.

2. Make train tracks leading to the entrance of the party using chalk or black electrical tape. Continue the train tracks throughout the party area. Put stops or "Stations" along your track. These stations can be located at each party activity. For example: Serve the refreshments at the "Restaurant Station." The "Mall" can be the station where you open the gifts. The "U-Make-It Shop" will be your craft area. "Games Galore" is the location where you will be playing the party games. Be sure to make signs for each station.

3. Paint several large boxes to resemble an engine, coal car, and caboose (see below). Glue on paper plates for the wheels. Stand a box on its side and attach it to the engine for the train cab. Cut windows in the sides and front of this box and use an empty oatmeal tub or coffee can for a smokestack. Fold construction paper into a triangle and attach to the engine to make the cowcatcher.

This large train may be used for various activities at the party. If sturdy enough, the children may play in the train cars. Store party favors and prizes in the coaches or caboose. Keep the coal car or engine empty to play the **Paddle the Balloon** game (see page 99).

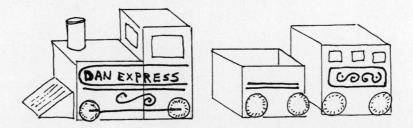

4. Make railroad crossing signs (see page 94) by attaching a wooden "X" to the top of a pole. On the "X" write "RAILROAD" (from the top left toward the bottom right) and "CROSSING" (from the bottom left toward the top right).

Attach a circle to the top of a pole (see above). Paint the circle white with a large black "X" on it. To the right and left of the "X" paint an "R."

REFRESHMENTS

"All Aboard" Cake: Use decorator frosting to draw train tracks around the top of a frosted 9-inch round layer cake. Accent with small plastic train cars on the tracks.

Circus Train Cookies:

    11 2½-inch square chocolate   decorator frosting
        covered graham crackers   2 packages ring-shaped
    11 animal crackers   hard candy

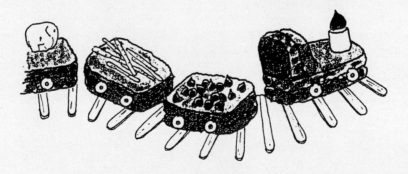

Frost the back of an animal cracker and attach to the center of a graham cracker (see above). Using a writing tip, pipe frosting around the outer edge of the graham cracker and pipe three vertical lines over the animal to resemble a cage. Attach two ring-shaped candies to the lower corners for the wheels. Arrange the cookies side by side to form a long train. Makes 11 cookies.

Individual Cake Trains: Prepare a covered cake board. Glue craft sticks onto the cake board to resemble train tracks (see below). Purchase one Suzy Q for each guest. Place them on the tracks to represent the cars. Frost each Suzy Q and decorate with chocolate candies in the "coal car," pretzel logs on a "flat car," animal crackers in the "box car," etc. Cut one Suzy Q in half, and place it on the rear side of the "engine." Place a large marshmallow on the engine with a chocolate candy on top for the smokestack. Use ring-shaped hard candy for wheels on each of the train cars.

Party Pizzas:

2 loaves party rye bread	1 pound pork sausage
1 pound processed American cheese	3 tablespoons chili sauce
	2 teaspoons oregano
8 ounces shredded mozzarella cheese	dash of garlic powder to taste

Brown the sausage. Melt the processed cheese in a double boiler or in a microwave. Mix all ingredients together and spread onto the rye bread. These can be frozen until ready to bake. Bake frozen pizzas for 10 to 12 minutes at 350 degrees.

PARTY FAVORS

- Decorate shoe boxes to resemble freight cars and fill with treats.
- Place the party favors in the center of a red bandana and tie the four corners together on a stick.
- *Suggested favors:* train postcards or photos, wooden train whistles, engineer hats, plastic train toys, travel items associated with a trip on the train.

CRAFTS

Shoe Box Engine:

2 shoe boxes (one with a lid)

4 poster board circles or small plastic lids

1 8″ × 11″ sheet of construction paper

1 4-inch cardboard tube

cotton balls

Stand the open shoe box on end and insert the second shoe box into it (see below). Decorate the cardboard tube and glue it to the center of the shoe box lid for the smokestack. Glue two circles on each side of the "engine" for wheels. Glue on squares of white paper for windows. To make the cowcatcher, fanfold the construction paper with 1-inch pleats. Fold under the end of the fan about one inch and use the lid of the shoe box to secure it in place. Draw or glue decorations on the engine and place cotton balls on the smokestack.

Train Whistles: Give each child a 3″ × 11″ piece of construction paper to decorate as he wishes. Wrap the paper around an empty 16-ounce soda bottle and tape in place. Tie a 2-foot piece of yarn around the neck of the bottle. Knot the ends of the yarn together, adjusting the length for the "whistle" to hang comfortably around the child's neck. Teach the children to blow across the top of the bottle to make it "toot" like a train whistle.

Suitcases: Cut a 1″ × 5″ strip from the center of one long side of a shirt box lid. Attach a piece of rope or yarn to the corresponding side of the box bottom, so that when the box is closed the rope loop will come through the opening in the lid. This rope is the handle of the suitcase. Use tape to "hinge" together the opposite side of the suitcase. Decorate the suitcase with travel labels, bumper stickers, or the children's drawings (see page 97).

During the party, as each child participates in an activity, he can receive an additional sticker for his suitcase.

U-Make-It Train:

1 11″ × 28″ piece of   glue
    poster board   markers or crayons
14 wooden craft sticks

Draw two horizontal lines, four inches apart, across the bottom of the poster board. Glue the craft sticks vertically between those lines, approximately two inches apart to make train tracks. Use the markers or crayons to draw scenery for background around the tracks.

Use these tracks to play the **U-Win-It Train** game (see below), or have poster board cutouts of train cars to glue on the tracks.

GAMES

U-Win-It Train: Prepare the **U-Make-It Train** craft (see above) at the beginning of the party to allow time for the glue to dry before playing the game.

For each person, cut from poster board one engine, one coal car, one passenger car, one freight car, and one caboose. Mix all these cars together and put them in a box.

Seat the children in a circle and have an adult pass the box around the circle, holding it above the children's heads to keep the contents out of sight. On his turn, a child will pick one car out of the box and place it on his track. If it is a duplicate, he will return it to the box. Play continues until each child has one each of the five different types of train cars. The children may then decorate and glue them onto their track.

Engine Hop: The children can make a human train by standing in a line and holding the waist of the child in front of them. Move to the music of the "Bunny Hop" singing the following song:

Get your engine started,
People all aboard,
Do the locomotion,
Chug, chug, chug.

Chuga-Chuga-Toot-Toot: Seat the children in a circle. One child is "it." This child walks around the outer edge of the circle, touching each child lightly on the head, and saying "Chuga." He will then choose one child and tap him on the head and say "Toot-Toot." This child will chase the first child around the circle, trying to tag him before he sits in the vacated spot. The second child then becomes "it." Continue the game until everyone has had a turn to be "it."

Race to the Station: This game requires a scoreboard. The scoreboard can be made on a sheet of poster board. Draw two sets of train tracks across the length of the poster board. Draw a train station at the top of each track. Tape a picture of a train to the bottom of each track.

Cover a tabletop with egg carton bottoms or muffin tins. Randomly paint the insides of the egg cups with assorted colors (or line the muffin tins with assorted colored baking cups).

Divide the children into two teams. The first player tosses a small ball into the egg cartons. If the ball lands in a red cup, the team moves its train up one track. If it lands in a blue cup, the train is moved up two tracks. If the ball lands in a yellow cup, the train remains in the same position. Players on both teams take turns tossing and moving the train up the track. The goal is to be the first team to reach the station at the top of the track.

Variation: Color one cup black. This represents a tunnel. If the ball is tossed into the tunnel, the train moves backward one space.

Whistle a Message: The children will stand on a line at one end of the party area facing you. You will stand at the opposite side with a train whistle. Explain to the children how different ways of whistling send different messages from the train. In this game, different whistles will send different messages to the children. One long blast will mean the children are to run ahead. One short blast will mean to stop. Two short blasts means to hop forward.

Begin sending your whistle messages. Anyone who moves incorrectly to the whistle will go back to the starting line. The first child to cross the finish line at the opposite side is the winner and can use his whistle to send the messages for the next round of play.

Pack the Suitcase: The children will need the suitcases they made during craft time. Their goal is to fill their suitcases with travel items. These may be the actual items or pictures of things that are packed in suitcases. Hide these items around the party area. Suggested items to hide are combs, toothbrushes, clothing, books, toy watches, hair spray, shoes, and toy cameras.

Instruct the children to find one of each item hidden. The first child to have fully packed his suitcase, without any duplicates, is the winner.

Variation: If you choose not to make the suitcases, this game can be played as a relay. Divide the group into two teams and give each team one piece of luggage. When the game begins, the first player on each team runs to find an item to bring to the suitcase. When he returns, the next child will hunt for an item. The first team to pack its suitcase wins.

Paddle the Balloon: For each team, make a paddle by taping a paint stir to a paper plate.

Divide the group into teams. Give each team member an inflated balloon. To begin, the first child on each team must bat the balloon with the paddle across the party area and into an empty train car (see Decorations, page 93). He will then run back to his team and hand off the paddle to the second child. The first team to have all its balloons in the train car is the winner. Be sure to have spare balloons on hand.

Construct a Train: Divide the group into teams. Give each team a diagram showing how to make a train engine with interlocking blocks (see below). Place the blocks onto a table approximately 15 feet from each team.

Each member of the team will take turns running to the table and returning with one block. The teammates will be constructing the engine to resemble the diagram. The first team to use all its blocks and to construct its train is the winner.

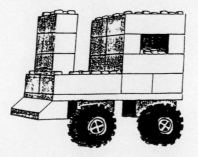

Pass the Prize: The children will sit in a circle. Give each child one wrapped prize. Read the children a story about a train. Instruct them that each time a certain word is said they will pass their prize to the person on their left. Be sure to use a word that is repeated often in the story, such as the name of the train or the lead character. At the end of the story the prize they are holding belongs to them to unwrap and enjoy.

Cowboy and Indian Party

INVITATIONS

- Cut two triangles from construction paper. Decorate one triangle to resemble an Indian tepee. Glue the decorated triangle to the other triangle along the edges leaving an opening for the door. Fold back the doorway to reveal the party information printed inside.
- Fold one piece of brown construction paper in half and cut into the shape of a cowboy boot (see below). Cut a spur shape from white construction paper and decorate with silver glitter. Glue the spur onto the boot.

DECORATIONS

Cowboy:

1. Make a horse drawn wagon for a centerpiece (see page 101). Remove the handle from a rectangular basket. Glue on four wagon wheels made from brown construction paper. Harness two plastic horses to the wagon with yarn or twine. Make small, individual wagons to match and fill with candy treats.

2. Make a rocking horse place card for each guest (see below). Fold a paper plate in half. Cut the shape of a horse from construction paper and glue to the side of the plate.

3. Draw western designs on a poster board. As each guest arrives he can autograph the poster and write a short saying. The birthday child will have a keepsake of his party.

4. A "town jail" can be made from a large, appliance-sized box. Cut a door in the back and bars for the window in the front. Take pictures of your guests in jail.

5. Place wagons, hobby horses, and rocking horses in front of the town jail.

Indian:

1. Decorate inverted sno-cone cups to resemble Indian tepees. Glue toothpicks in the top for poles. Write each child's name on a tepee to use as place cards. Hide a small treat under each tepee for an extra surprise.

2. Make a totem pole by decorating four boxes that are the same size with Indian designs. Stack the boxes on top of each other and glue together (see right).

3. Indian canoes can be made as centerpieces or as individual party favors. Cut and fold a poster board as shown (see below). Tape together to form the canoe and fill with candy.

4. Decorate the face of each guest with "war paint" using acrylic waterbase paint.

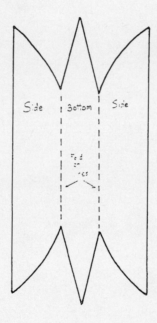

REFRESHMENTS

Corral Cake: Bake your favorite cake mix in a 9″ × 13″ pan. Let cool and frost. For the corral, insert toothpicks (for fence posts) around the outer edge of the cake. Wrap yarn from fence post to fence post. Place small plastic animals inside the corral.

"Burger 'n' Fries": *Burgers:* Between two vanilla wafers (buns), place green frosting (pickle), a chocolate candy (hamburger), and red frosting (catsup).

French fries: Cut graham crackers into ½-inch strips. Serve them in a french fry bag with red frosting (catsup) on the side.

Trail Mix

¼ cup melted margarine
3 teaspoons Worcestershire
  sauce
4 cups Corn Chex
4 cups Wheat Chex
8 ounces unsalted dry
  roasted peanuts
6 ounces pretzel sticks.

Combine the margarine and Worcestershire sauce in a small bowl. Mix the remaining ingredients and place on a cookie sheet. Pour sauce over mixture and stir until evenly coated. Bake at 250 degrees for 15 minutes, remove and stir, and bake 15 more minutes.

If desired, add the following ingredients after baking: sunflower seeds, popcorn, raisins, or peanut butter chips.

Campfires For each "campfire" you will need the following items:

1 napkin or plate to represent
  your "cleared off area"
1 small cup to represent
  the "water bucket"
½ cup corn pops cereal
  for the "rocks"
3 log pretzel sticks for
  the "logs"
1 tablespoon coconut for
  the "tinder"
5 thin pretzel sticks for
  the "kindling"
1 candy corn for the
  "matchhead"
1 toothpick for the
  "matchhead"
5 red hots to act as the
  "burning fire"

Instruct the children to prepare their campfires. First, they will need a cleared off area. Make sure everyone has a water bucket ready, filled with water. Next, they will place their rocks in a circle on their cleared off area. Place the logs in an "A" shaped pattern inside the circle of rocks. Sprinkle the tinder inside the "A" shape and slant the kindling across the logs.

Place the match head onto the match stick and tell each child to strike his match against a rock to light the fire. Sprinkle the red hots on top of the fire and watch the fire blaze. After eating their fire, the children should put the fire out with their water buckets.

Outdoor Cooking: Place hot dogs and marshmallows onto sticks and roast over an open fire. Serve on pie tins.

S'Mores For each "S'More" layer (sandwich style):

1 graham cracker (bottom)
2 jumbo marshmallows
  (melted over the fire, if desired)
1 chocolate candy bar
1 graham cracker (top)

PARTY FAVORS

• Purchase one red bandana for each child. Place the treats inside the bandana and tie all four corners together with rope.

• Make horse drawn wagons (see Decorations, page 100) to hold the party favors.

• Decorate a paper bag with Indian symbols (see below). Personalize the bags with the guest's **Indian Name** (see Games, page 109).

• *Suggested favors*: sheriff badges, Lone Ranger mask, cap guns or water guns, holsters, slingshots, canteens or water bottles, Indian headdress, bow and arrows, tomahawks, peace pipes (bubble pipes).

CRAFTS

Cowboy Hats: Purchase white, plastic cowboy hats from your local craft or novelty store. Give the children permanent markers and allow them to personalize and decorate the hats. Suggest drawing a cactus, a sun, a horse, or boots.

Holsters:

2 pieces of vinyl fabric cut into triangular shapes	vinyl or plastic lacing
	1 36-inch rope

Prepunch holes, one inch apart, around the edges of the vinyl fabric. Lace the two pieces of vinyl fabric together, leaving them open at the top. Cut two slits into the top of the back triangle. Thread the rope through the slits and tie the rope around the child's waist. Give each child a water gun to put into his holster.

Cowboy and Indian Wrestlers: Give each child two wooden clothespins and markers. Decorate one clothespin to resemble an Indian and the other clothespin to resemble a cowboy (see below). Put one strong rubber band around the cowboy and the Indian. Twist the rubber band around until it is very tight. Drop them on the floor and watch them wrestle.

Totem Poles: Each child will need three white paper cups and two 4-inch circles of poster board. Use markers to decorate each inverted cup with Indian faces and designs. Glue two cups onto the circles. Stack them together and glue in place. Make a feather headdress from construction paper and glue onto the top (see below).

Indian Headdress: Cut poster board into a 1″ × 22″ strip. Cut slits in the strip as shown above. Decorate the center of the band using markers or crayons. Staple the ends together. Offer a choice of assorted colored feathers to insert into the slits.

Indian Vests: Cut a slit up the center of a brown paper grocery bag. Cut a neck hole and two armholes to make a vest. The children will draw Indian symbols on the vests and cut fringe up from the bottom of the bag (see below). When they have completed their vests, they may want to crumple them and smooth them out to give them the appearance of animal hides.

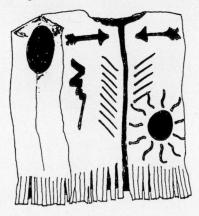

Indian Necklaces: Prior to the party, make a variety of colored mostaccoli noodles by soaking the noodles in a mixture of ¼ cup rubbing alcohol and one teaspoon food coloring. Cut one 30-inch piece of yarn or string for each child. Direct the children to string the noodles onto the yarn and tie the yarn together at the ends. Noodles can be alternated with ring-shaped hard candy if desired.

GAMES

Shoot the Target: Make a slingshot for each guest by bending the sides of a coat hanger to form a "V" shape. Bend the hook toward the center and wrap with tape to cover any sharp points. Use a strong rubber band to shoot (see below).

Prepare a target for each guest, by drawing three circles on an 11" × 14" piece of poster board. If time permits, allow the children to color their targets. Number each circle for points.

Stand the finished targets against a wall. Give the children crumpled sheets of newspaper or foam balls to shoot at their targets.

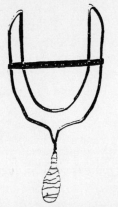

Lasso to Win: Make lassos by covering embroidery hoops with rope or by stiffening a rope with liquid starch to hold a circular shape. Gather six stuffed animals for each team. On each animal place one number ranging from one to six.

Divide the children into teams. The children will lasso the stuffed animals. Use the numbers as points, and the team which lassos the most points is the winner.

Variation: Use prewrapped prizes in place of animals. The child will keep the prize he lassos.

Wheelbarrow Race: Divide the guests into pairs behind a starting line. The back child in the pair will hold up the legs of the front child (who is now walking on his hands). When the race begins each pair must travel to a line with one child holding up the other's legs. When they cross the line the pairs switch positions and travel back to the starting line. The first pair to cross the starting line wins.

Sharpshooters: Divide the group into two teams. Give each child on team one (Indians) peace pipes (bubble pipes) and bubbles. Give each child on team two (cowboys) a loaded water gun. The goal for the cowboys is to shoot the Indians' bubbles, before any of them hit the ground. After a few minutes of play, switch roles so everyone will have a chance to blow bubbles and to shoot.

Pan for Gold: Punch holes in pie tins. Position the children around a sandbox or tub of water. Give each child a tin and have him pan for pennies. Be sure to have enough pennies for each child to collect a minimum of ten.

Indian Attack: Make a "corral" in your party area by placing stakes into the ground six to eight feet apart in a large circle. String rope or crepe paper streamers from stake to stake to enclose the corral. (For an indoor party, tape a circle to the floor of the game area.)

Divide the children into two teams. Name the teams the "Cowboys" and the "Indians." The Cowboys will stand inside the corral. The Indians will stand around the outside of the corral. Give each team plenty of ammunition. Ammunition can be foam balls, table tennis balls, crumpled newspaper balls, etc.

Set a timer for one minute. When you say "Go," the Indians attack the Cowboys by throwing their ammunition into the corral. The Cowboys fight back by throwing the ammo out at the Indians. Everyone will stop when the timer goes off and will count the ammunition inside and outside the corral. The team to have landed the most ammo in the other team's area wins. Set the timer and begin again. Continue for several rounds.

Variation: Give ammunition (a play ball) only to the Indians. They will attack the Cowboys who will be dodging the ammo. Any Cowboy who is hit will leave the corral as a "captive" of the Indians and will become an Indian trying to hit his former teammates. The last Cowboy remaining in the corral is the winner. The teams can switch sides and play again.

Ride and Shoot: Divide the children into two teams. Give each team a stick horse and each child a water gun.

The first child on each team rides the horse across the party area and around the corral. (Team one rides clockwise and team two rides counterclockwise.) As the two riders pass each other going around the corral, they will shoot each other with the water guns and then ride back to start. At the start line, they pass the horse to the next teammate who will ride and shoot the opponent. Continue until all children have had a turn.

Suggestion: While watching their teammate ride and shoot, the other children can be yelling Indian war cries or can be beating an Indian drum beat on their legs.

Rainmaker: Seat the children in a circle "Indian style." Let the birthday child be the "rainmaker." He starts the sounds listed below, in order, and the person next to him joins in, continuing around the circle. When the sound gets back to the rainmaker, he begins the next sound. As the sounds build, it will seem as if you are listening to a rainstorm.

a) Rub the thumb against the first two fingers.
b) Slowly rub the palms of the hands together.
c) Rub hands up and down the thighs.
d) Pat the knees with the hands, increasing in speed.
e) Rapidly tap feet against the ground.

Reverse the order to end the storm. If played outside, mist the children with a spray water bottle.

Indian Name Game: As each child arrives, he is given an Indian name that is used throughout the entire party. Begin the party by playing charades. Each child will act out his Indian name for the others to guess. Here are a few suggested names: Running Deer, Laughing Eyes, Dances with Wolves, Stands with Trees, Bright as Sun, Brave Horse, Kicking Mule, Sleeps with Bears.

Follow the Footprints: In this game the "Indians" track their party favors. Place sets of "footprints" throughout the party area. On each set of footprints, write the name of one of the "Indians." (There must be a set of footprints for each child.) Each child will follow his footprints to his prize.

The Powwow: To end this party, gather the guests around the "campfire" and have them listen to cowboy and Indian stories, smoke peace pipes (bubble pipes), and sing campfire songs, such as "Home on the Range."

Football Party

INVITATIONS

• Fold a sheet of brown construction paper in half. Cut out a football shape being careful not to cut on the fold line. Decorate the outside with stitches and stripes to resemble a football. Print the necessary invitation information on the inside of the football.

• Draw nine equally spaced yard lines and end zones with a white marker across a green sheet of construction paper. Write, at the ends of each line, the numbers 10, 20, 30, 40, 50, 40, 30, 20, 10 and draw goalposts at each end of the "field." Write the invitation information on the yard lines.

DECORATIONS

1. Make a ticket booth by cutting a door into the back of a large, appliance-sized box to use as the entrance to the booth. Cut a window in the front of the booth. Hang a "Ticket Booth" sign at the top of the booth. Decorate the booth with football posters and pennants or with your own football drawings (see right).

At the beginning of the party, have the birthday child stand inside the booth and welcome his guests to the party. Tickets to be "admitted" to the party can be delivered to the guests with their invitations or give them tickets as they arrive. If the tickets are sent with the invitations, be sure to have extras on hand for those who forget to bring them.

When it is time for refreshments, change the sign on the booth to read "Concession Stand." The guests can go to the concession stand to "purchase" their treats. Give the guests tickets or play money so they can pay for their purchases.

2. Goalposts can be made by taping together wrapping paper rolls, using heavy masking tape (see below). Cut a hole the diameter of the roll in a box. Insert each roll into the box for support. Stand the goal posts at opposite ends of the party area.

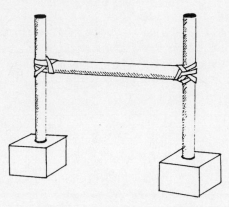

3. Write the numbers 10, 20, 30, 40, and 50 onto paint stirs. Place these into the ground to mark the yard lines.

4. To make a scoreboard (see below), cut a 3″ × 3″ hole on both the right and left side of a sheet of poster board. From a contrasting sheet of poster board, cut two 12-inch circles and write numbers around the edges of each. Insert a brad to connect each circle to the scoreboard. Be sure a number is visible through the hole. This number will be the team score. Label the top of each side with a team name. The circle can be rotated to change the score during the scrimmage.

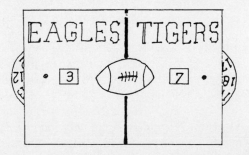

5. Hang pennant flags of professional football teams on the wall. These can be made from construction paper or felt and given as party favors.

6. Adults helping with the party can dress as referees or cheerleaders. One adult can be the party sportscaster. With a cordless microphone he can give a play-by-play report of the party events.

7. Apply black "grease" under the eyes of the party guests so they will resemble football players.

REFRESHMENTS

Football Cake: Bake your favorite cake mix in a 9″ × 13″ pan. Cut a football shape as shown below. Frost with chocolate frosting, mounding the frosting slightly towards the middle. Decorate with licorice laces and candy coated chocolates.

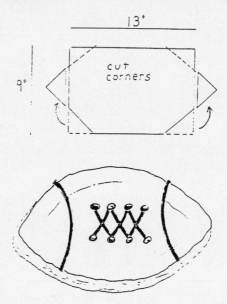

Frozen Football Fields: Slice 1-inch-thick slices from a half-gallon carton of vanilla ice cream. Cover the slice with green sprinkles. Place four 5-inch licorice laces across the field for yard lines. Top with a chocolate football. Makes 7 servings.

Caramel Apples: Cut apples into bite-sized pieces. Top with caramel topping. Serve in small, plastic football helmets.

Pigs in a Blanket: Divide a package of refrigerated crescent rolls into eight triangles. Roll one cocktail wiener inside each crescent dough and bake at 375 degrees for 10 minutes, or until golden brown.

Steaming Drinks: Serve each guest a mug of hot chocolate. Top with marshmallows.

PARTY FAVORS

- Package the party favors inside a toy football helmet.
- Place party favors in penalty flags (squares of yellow fabric) and tie the four corners together.
- Make your own party favor bags by stitching together two pieces of brown felt, cut into the shape of a football. Be sure to leave an opening at the top to fill. Use a permanent marker to draw the stripes and lacing.
- *Suggested favors:* whistles, toy footballs, chocolate candies wrapped in football foil, football trading cards, trophies, posters of football players, player figurines.

CRAFTS

Field Goal Game: Cut a large football shape from the center of a paper plate (see below). Draw a goalpost on the plate. Tape the plate with masking tape to a stick. (A paint stir works well.) Cut a 24-inch piece of string and tie one end to the stick and the other end to a small toy football. The children will try to toss the small football through the hole to make a "goal."

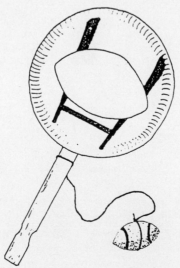

Let the Band Play: During "halftime," everyone can make a musical instrument to play in the marching band.

DRUMS—Cover empty oatmeal tubs with white paper. Have the children color and decorate them. Beat with a pencil.

SHAKERS—Let the children decorate the bottom of two paper plates. Place beans inside and staple the plates together.

TAMBOURINES—Decorate tin pie plates with stickers. Punch holes in the plate and attach several jingle bells with ribbon.

Football Souvenirs: Pennants and **Card Collector's Album** (see Baseball Party Crafts, page 119) would also be fun crafts to make at this party.

GAMES

Calisthenics: A football party should begin with warm-up calisthenics. Blow the whistle to begin a new movement.

Suggestions: jog forward then back, run through tires, do jumping jacks, run side to side, do sit-ups, do push-ups, do arm circles, do stretches, etc.

Number Game: Tape a number on the back of each guest's shirt, similar to the numbers that football players have on their jerseys. The object of the game is for each child to guess what his number is, by asking questions such as "Is my number higher than 10?"; "Is my number lower than 40?"; "Do you know a professional player who wears this number?"; "What team does he play for?" The first child to guess his number is the winner.

Number Hunt: Tape numbers onto small toy footballs that correspond to numbers taped onto the children's backs. Hide the footballs around the party area. The children will hunt for the ball that matches their number. They can then keep the ball as a party favor.

Scrimmage: Divide the children into two teams for a football scrimmage. To avoid injuries, have the players touch their opponents instead of tackling them. Flip a coin to see who has control of the ball. Suggest that the teams huddle between plays to determine if they will pass, run or punt the ball. You can control the length of the scrimmage by setting a timer to go off at halftime and at the end of the game. Mark the field with goalposts at each end. These can be made from two poles with crepe paper tied from pole to pole.

Videotape the game and end your party by watching the instant replays of the scrimmage.

Point Grid: On poster board, draw nine lines across and nine lines down to make a grid. Randomly write the numbers zero through nine across the top of the grid and down one side of the grid. Write one team's name across the top and the other team's name along the side.

As each arrives at the party, he will sign his name in a square on the point grid. During the **Scrimmage** (see page 114), after each quarter is played, refer to the chart. The child whose name corresponds to the last digit of each team's score wins a prize.

Trivia Scrimmage: Divide the children into two teams. Have the teams go to opposite ends of the room and sit in a row facing the other team. Use white crepe paper streamers for the yard lines between the two teams.

Place a football on the yard line in front of each team. Ask each team football trivia questions. Be sure to gear your questions toward the age level and skills of the group. A correct answer advances the ball to the next yard line. Alternate the questions between teams until a team has advanced the football across the last yard line to score a touchdown.

Sample trivia questions:

a) How many points does a team get when scoring a touchdown? (six points)
b) How many points does a team get when kicking a field goal? (three points)
c) How many players from each team are on the field? (11 players)
d) What professional team's home is in Chicago? (Bears)
e) What football player is nicknamed the "Refrigerator"? (William Perry)
f) What color is the penalty flag? (yellow)

Touchdown Race: Use white tape for yard lines across the floor. The children will sit in a row facing the "field." Give the children toy footballs. Have them place the footballs on the yard line closest to them. At the sound of the whistle each child pushes the ball across the field with his nose. The first child to score a touchdown is the winner.

Kick a Field Goal: Divide the children into two teams. Give the first player on each team a football. He will have one turn to try to kick the ball directly over a goal. Each time a team member kicks a field goal, that team will score one point. Continue playing for several rounds. The team scoring the most points is the winner.

Passing Practice: Tie a large hoop to a pole mounted into the ground. Stand the children at a premarked distance (a "yard line") away from the hoop. Give each child one turn to pass the football through the hoop, increasing the distance to be thrown (an additional yard line) after each successful pass.

Placing several hoops in the yard will reduce waiting and give everyone plenty of turns.

Leap and Hike: Divide the children into teams. Line up each team, leaving ample space for "leaping" between each player. All the children will squat low to the ground. Give the last child in each row a football. That child will carry the football under his arm and leap over each teammate until he is at the front of the row. He will then hike the football between his legs to the second person, and all the players will continue to hike the ball back until it is in the hands of the last player in the row. This player will then begin leaping forward. Play continues until each person has leaped over all the other players. The children should then be in their original order. The first team to finish is the winner.

Pass the Football: Divide the children into pairs. Each child will stand in his own circle (made with yarn or string) with the partners facing each other. Give each pair of children one football. The partners will pass the ball back and forth to each other. They are not allowed to go out of their circle to pass or to receive. If they do, drop a yellow penalty flag into the circle. The partners with the least amount of flags are the winners.

Baseball Party

INVITATIONS

• Using construction paper, cut approximately six tickets for each guest. On the first ticket write all necessary invitation information. On the other tickets write the following:

> one admission to David's birthday party
> good for one hot dog
> good for one ice cream cone
> admit one to the **Punch Ball** game (see page 120)
> admit one to the **Baseball Card Hunt** (see page 121)

The guests should bring these tickets to the party. An usher can direct the guests to the ticket booth at your party entrance as they arrive. Be sure to have extra tickets on hand for those guests who forget to bring theirs.

• Cut the shape of a baseball glove from brown construction paper (see below). Fold a piece of white construction paper in half. Cut out a baseball shape being careful not to cut on the fold line. Glue to the glove and print the necessary information on the inside of the baseball.

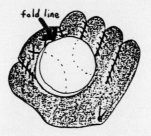

DECORATIONS

1. Decorate a ticket booth (see Football Party Decorations, page 110).

117

2. Make the party area into a baseball diamond. Be sure the bases are secure on the ground and include a pitcher's mound. Place a bench on each side of the field for the dugouts.

3. Accent the party area with gloves, balls, trophies, hats, bats, posters, and pennants.

4. Make place mats that are designed to look like scorecards (see below). List the guests' names as the players on a 12″ × 18″ sheet of construction paper. Cover with clear Contact paper.

No.	Pos	PLAYER	1	2	3	4	5	6	7	8	9
10	RP	Mark									
36	P	Dan									
12	FB	Rick									
18	TB	David									
23	SS	Eric									
9	LF	Mike									
8	CF	Ray									
11	SB	Tim									
16	C	Andy									
		TOTAL R/H									

5. Apply black "grease" under the eyes of the party guests to make them resemble baseball players.

6. Adults at the party could dress like umpires, wearing navy blue or black shirts and pants. Do not forget the hat.

REFRESHMENTS

Diamond Cake: Bake your favorite cake mix in two 9-inch square pans. Layer and frost with chocolate frosting for the infield and green frosting for the outfield. Decorate with candy for the bases and plastic player figurines.

Home Run Ice Cream: Place a scoop of ice cream between two large sugar cookies. Press cookies gently together to make an ice cream sandwich. Pipe baseball stitches onto the top with decorator frosting.

Nachos: Melt two pounds of nacho-flavored cheese in a crockpot. Pour a scoop over individual plates of tortilla chips.

Grand-Slam: Serve refreshments normally purchased at a baseball game, such as hot dogs, peanuts, popcorn, Cracker Jacks, or soft pretzels.

PARTY FAVORS

- Package party favors inside of megaphones or batting helmets.
- Decorate shoe boxes to resemble sport lockers and fill with party favors (see below).

- Stitch together the long sides of two felt pennants for a party favor bag.
- *Suggested favors:* baseball cards, baseball gum, trophies, chocolate candy wrapped in baseball foil, Baby Ruth candy bars, posters of baseball players, player figurines.

CRAFTS

Pennants: Cut a wooden dowel to approximately thirty inches in length. Cut white felt in the shape of a pennant. Fold over the short side of the triangle and sew or glue a seam. Insert the dowel through the seam and secure with glue. Use markers to decorate the pennants with the children's favorite team name or an original design.

Baseball Caps: Purchase baseball caps, preferably void of any logo or design. The "baseball players" can decorate them with fabric markers. Let the children wear the caps throughout the party.

Card Collector's Album:

1 folder with pockets and 3 brads	2 plastic baseball card sheets with 2½" × 3½"
baseball stickers	slip-in pockets
markers	baseball cards

Give each child a folder and allow him to decorate it with stickers and markers to create his own personal card collector's album. Insert the plastic sheets into the folder brads. Slide the baseball cards into the plastic pockets. The pockets in the folder can be used to hold other party favors.

GAMES

Baseball Game: No matter what the ages of the children, they can play baseball. For children ages five and up, play the game on a baseball diamond with an adult as the pitcher. Indicate on the invitation that guests should bring a glove. For younger children, a batting tee can be used to replace pitching. Tee ball is similar to baseball, except the batter swings at a stationary ball instead of a moving pitch.

Establishing some "house" rules may add to everyone's enjoyment of the game, regardless of skill level. For example, during an inning all players on each team will get one turn to bat. Or, set a maximum run limit to keep the games evenly matched.

If a team scores the maximum number of runs allowed in an inning, before making three outs, it will be the other team's turn to bat. Do not count strikes or balls, but pitch to each child until he gets a hit. Do not allow base stealing.

Indoor Baseball: Tie a whiffle ball to a string and hang it from the ceiling. When the batter hits the ball, he will run to first base, hop to second base, skip to third base, and run backwards to home plate. With this activity everyone gets a home run as long as he remembers to move correctly from base to base.

Punch Ball: Play this variation of baseball with an inflated play ball. The players use their arms as the bat. The pitcher bounces the ball to the batter. The batter then punches it with his fist. The rules of baseball apply, except the fielders may get the base runners out by throwing the ball at their feet. If the runner is hit by the ball, he is out.

Game Highlights: To begin your baseball game, announce the names and positions of the players on both teams. You may wish to sing "The Star Spangled Banner."

In the seventh inning have everyone sit down for the "seventh inning stretch" and take a break. This may be a good time for refreshments and to teach the activities created by fans at different stadiums, such as the following:

THE WAVE CHEER—seat everyone to form a circle. The first person will stand and raise both hands high above his head and then lower them and sit back down. Immediately following him, the second person does the same, followed by the third, and so on. Continue back to the first child and repeat again. Practice a few times to get it running smoothly.

Sing "Take Me Out to the Ballgame"

Baseball Card Flips: Divide the guests into groups. As the children stand in a circle, have the first child flip his baseball card onto the floor. The person on his left flips one card trying to get his card to land on top of the first player's card. If he succeeds, he gets to keep the cards lying on the floor. If his card does not touch another card, the next player proceeds to flip his card, again trying to touch one of the cards already on the floor. This continues until a player's card has landed on a card. You may wish to set a timer to determine when the playing will end, or call an end to the game when the cards are fairly evenly distributed among the guests.

Baseball Card Hunt: Hide baseball cards around the party area. Each child must find only one each of the following positions: pitcher, catcher, infielder, and outfielder (for older children you can be more specific and find all nine positions). The hunt continues until all children have found one card for each position. For nonreaders, premark the baseball cards with alphabet stickers in the corner. Each guest must find one each of "P" (pitcher), "C" (catcher), "I" (infielder) and "O" (outfielder).

Statistic Game: After playing the **Baseball Card Hunt** (see above), each child will use his cards to play this "Statistic Game."

From poster board, make a large scorecard or graph with each of the guest's name on it.

Every child with a baseball card that matches the question will receive one point on the scorecard.

Sample questions:

a) Who has a pitcher who has won more than 20 games in one year?
b) Who has an infielder with more than a .300 batting average?
c) Who has a player that has played for more than two teams?
d) Who has a rookie?
e) Who has a pitcher with an ERA under 3.00?
f) Who has a pitcher with an ERA over 3.00?

Hot Box: Divide the children into groups of three. Two children will be standing at the bases, which are approximately 25 feet from each other. The third child is the runner. The basemen will throw a ball back and forth while the runner tries to run across to the other base without being tagged out. If out, he becomes a baseman and the next child is a runner.

Base Stealing Relay: Cut three cardboard bases for each child (first, second and third base). Stack these bases at each base position on a baseball diamond.

Divide the group into two teams. Each team lines up at home plate, facing the baseball diamond. The first child in each line runs to first base, "steals" it by picking it up, and runs back to home plate. The next child in line runs directly to second base, picks up a base and returns to home. The third child in line runs to third base, steals a base, and returns home. Play continues until all bases have been stolen and brought home. The first team to finish wins.

Interpret the Hand Signals: Tell the children how coaches will often use hand signals to tell their players what to do during a game. Being able to remember and follow these hand signals is important for playing games.

Teach several hand signals and use them to play a variation of "Simon Says." Suggested signals:

Leader:	*Players:*
touches ear	swing like a batter
tips cap	run to the baseline
touches nose	clap and cheer like the fans
rubs stomach	walk to the dugout

Baseball Pinata: Blow up one large balloon in the shape of a ball. Cut strips of newspaper approximately ½" × 18". Mix together equal amounts of flour and water. Dip the strips of newspaper into the mixture one at a time. Using your thumb and forefinger squeeze the excess amount of mixture from the newspaper strip. Wrap it around the balloon and smooth flat. Repeat until the balloon has approximately two coats of newspaper. The more newspaper applied, the stronger the pinata will be. Let dry overnight.

After the pinata is dry, paint it white. Let dry again and then paint the black stitches around the baseball pinata.

Pop the balloon with a knife and cut a small opening in the pinata. Fill it with candy and small prizes. Tie with string and hang it in the party area.

To play the game, have the guests stand in a line. Blindfold (if desired) the first person and give him a plastic bat. He will swing the bat and try to hit the pinata. Be sure to keep the other guests out of range of the swinging bat.

Each person gets one swing at the pinata, trying to break it open. Once the baseball has been broken open all the children may run and pick up the candy and prizes.

Halloween Party

INVITATIONS

• Fold a piece of orange construction paper in half. Draw a spider web with a black marker. Punch several holes in a piece of black construction paper using a hole punch. Glue the black dots onto the spider web and draw on legs to make spiders (see below).

• Fold a piece of white construction paper in half and cut out a ghost shape (see below). Do not cut on the fold line. Cut out eyes and a mouth from the top sheet. On the inside of the ghost, write "BOO," so it is showing through the mouth. Finish writing, "Boo Hoo, I'll be sad if you can't come to my party on October 31...."

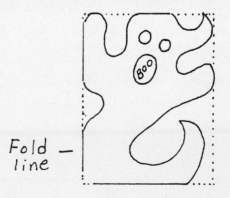

DECORATIONS

1. Hang inflated balloons from the ceiling with string. Tape party plates to paint stirs for paddles. Children will enjoy bopping the balloons while waiting for other guests to arrive. Be sure to keep the balloons a safe distance apart.

2. In a corner of the room, string a large spider web from wall to wall. Place plastic spiders in the web for authenticity.

3. To make a ghost, inflate a balloon, drape a white sheet over the balloon, and tie with a string. Tape two, black construction paper eyes onto the ghost. Hang the ghost from the ceiling.

4. Stuff clothing with newspaper or straw to make a scarecrow. Use a plastic pumpkin bucket for a head. Place him on a bench. Let the party guests sit next to him and take their picture.

5. Invert a brown paper bag and cut out a pumpkin face on the side. Place a flashlight inside and watch your pumpkin glow.

REFRESHMENTS

Pumpkin Cake: Decorate a round layer cake to look like a pumpkin face by frosting the cake orange and accenting it with green and black frosting.

Munch a Spider: For each spider you will need one Hostess Ding Dong and two black pipe cleaners. Cut the pipe cleaners into 3-inch pieces to make eight legs. Bend the legs into a "Z" shape and insert four legs into each side of the Ding Dong (see below).

Caramel Apples: Cut apples into slices and place in individual serving dishes. Pour caramel topping over the apples. Add nuts if desired.

Popcorn Balls:

12 cups popcorn (approximately ½ cup unpopped)
1 cup light corn syrup
1 cup sugar
½ teaspoon salt
1 teaspoon vanilla

Spray a large roasting pan with cooking spray. Add popped corn. Keep warm in a 250 degree oven until the candy coating is ready.

Cook corn syrup, sugar, and salt over medium heat, stirring frequently, until mixture comes to a full boil. Cook without stirring for 7 minutes. Remove from heat and stir in vanilla. Slowly pour over popcorn, stirring until evenly coated. Cool popcorn, stirring, just until mixture can be handled. Immediately grease hands with margarine and quickly shape into popcorn balls. Makes seven 4-inch balls.

Gummy Worm Special: Fill clear plastic glasses with orange flavored gelatin. Place two gummy worms into each glass and chill until almost firm. Place two more gummy worms into the gelatin, draping them over the side of the glass.

Fruity Pumpkin Pizza:

1 package refrigerated sugar cookie dough
8 ounces cream cheese
8 ounces nondairy whipped topping
1 teaspoon vanilla
orange food coloring
1 can peaches, drained and sliced thin
1 can mandarin oranges, drained
seedless grapes, sliced in half
sliced fresh strawberries

Spread the cookie dough into a lightly greased pizza pan. Bake at 350 degrees for 10 to 15 minutes, until golden brown. Cool.

Blend the cream cheese, whipped topping, vanilla, and food coloring and spread over the cookie. Chill until firm.

Top with the fruit, as shown below, decorating the pizza to resemble a jack-o'-lantern.

strawberries
peaches
grapes
oranges

Witch Mix: Prepare a "Witches' Cookbook" to use as a visual aid. Cover a hardback book with a book cover. Decorate and title the book cover "Witches' Cookbook."

Place a large caldron in the center of the room. Give each child one ingredient for making the "Witch Mix." As you call for each spooky ingredient, the children will put it into the pot. After all ingredients are added, stir with a wooden spoon until well mixed. Serve each child a scoop of the "Witch Mix."

Suggested ingredients: vampire fangs (candy corn), ghost guts (popcorn), skeleton bones (pretzel logs), eyeballs (small round candies), dried worms (Chinese noodles), tongue (cut from a fruit roll-up)

PARTY FAVORS

Sucker Ghosts: Wrap one white facial tissue around a sucker to resemble a ghost. Tie black yarn around the "neck" of the ghost and let the tissue hang down along the stick. Draw on eyes with a black marker.

Ghost Puppets: Cut two ghost shapes from white felt. Sew or glue with tacky glue around all sides of the ghost, leaving an opening at the bottom for your hand. Glue on two eyes, cut from black felt. Fill with goodies.

Pumpkin Goody Bags (see below):

    a) Cut two pieces of orange felt with pinking shears, in the shape of an 8-inch pumpkin.
    b) Glue the orange felt together around the outside edges with tacky glue, leaving the top open.
    c) Cut two leaves from green felt and glue to the front and back of the pumpkin.
    d) Cut eyes, nose, and mouth from black felt and glue them onto the pumpkin.
    e) Glue on a 1" × 11" strip of green felt for the handle.

Halloween Flashlights: Purchase one flashlight for each child. These will be used in the **Spook House** game (see page 131), or if desired, these can be filled with candy and other treats.

Pumpkin Jars: Cut a rectangle from orange felt to wrap around a baby food jar. Glue into place with tacky glue. Cut a circle from green felt and glue onto the lid. Cut eyes, nose and a mouth from black felt and glue to the jar to make a jack-o'-lantern face. Fill the jar with candy corn and other sweet treats.

CRAFTS

Paint a Jack-o'-Lantern: Purchase one small pumpkin for each child. Give the guests a marker to outline a face on the pumpkin. Paint the face, using acrylic, waterbase paints.

Trick-or-Treat Pillowcase: A personalized trick-or-treat bag can be made from a white pillowcase. Line the inside of the pillowcase with newspaper. Draw an outline of a pumpkin, cat, or ghost on one side of the pillowcase and let the children color and decorate it. Offer several colors of fabric paints or fabric markers.

Pumpkin Magnet: Cut three pieces of orange felt, as illustrated below. Cut the leaf from green felt and the stem from brown felt. Glue the brown stem to the largest orange piece with tacky glue. Glue the second and third orange pieces on top. Cut a 4-inch piece of green pipe cleaner. Wrap the pipe cleaner around a pencil to curl it. Glue the pipe cleaner and green leaf to the top of the pumpkin, near the stem. Attach two moveable eyes. Glue a happy smile to the pumpkin, using black yarn. Attach a magnet strip to the back.

Wind Sock Ghost: Punch holes in the top of a 24″ × 18″ sheet of white construction paper, six inches from each end (see right). Place reinforcement labels at each hole to prevent tearing. Cut a 24-inch piece of yarn and tie through each hole to form the handle. Cut six white crepe paper streamers into 24-inch lengths.

Give the children black markers and let them draw a ghost face in the center of the paper. Turn the paper over and glue the streamers onto the bottom of the paper. Wrap the paper in a cylinder shape and glue or staple the seam.

Ghost Doorknob Cover: Cut the shape of a ghost from white felt (see below). Cut a 2-inch circle from the ghost for a mouth. Cut two ovals from black felt for eyes. Cut three 6-inch pieces of Halloween colored ribbon. Tie a bell onto the end of each ribbon. Glue the eyes and ribbons onto the ghost with tacky glue. Hang by the mouth over the doorknob.

Haunted House:

½ pint milk carton	assorted candy decorations
black spray paint	**Sucker Ghost** (see Party
orange construction paper	Favors, page 127)
foam tray	

Spray paint the milk carton black, leaving the pour spout open for the chimney. Glue the painted carton to the foam tray. Cut windows and a door from construction paper and glue onto the carton.

Decorate the haunted house using candy corn for shingles, black licorice for sidewalks and guttering, and candy pumpkins for yard decoration. Insert the **Sucker Ghost** (see page 127) into the chimney.

Create a Mask: Purchase an assortment of solid colored paper plates. Prepare one plate for each child by cutting holes into the plate large enough for full vision. Cut a 12-inch piece of elastic and staple the ends to each side of the plate.

The children can create their own masks, such as jack-o'-lanterns, clowns, and witches. Offer yarn, markers, construction paper, sequins, glitter, feathers, pipe cleaners, and pom-poms for decorating the masks.

GAMES

Witches' Brew: Fill individual Halloween goody bags with candy and place them in a large black caldron or kettle. Cover the bags with black tissue paper to create a false bottom.

At the beginning of the party, tell the children they are going to make "Witches' Brew" and give each child a special ingredient to place into the pot, such as a rabbit's foot, a cinnamon stick, a chicken bone, a garlic clove, a rock, a spider, candy corn, or plastic fangs. After the last ingredient is added, tell the children their brew must stew for a while to become their sweet treats. Set the pot to the side to be used later in the party.

When you are ready to hand out the party favors, have the hostess or teacher give the pot a stir. While stirring, the children should repeat the following:

"Witches and bats
Skeletons and cats
Make the brew
Just for you!"

The stirring will bring the favors to the top and push the black tissue to the bottom of the pot. When finished stirring, let the children look into the pot. It will be delightful to see their surprise and pleasure at the treats they have made.

Skeleton Bones: Make a "coffin," using a rectangular box, spray painted black. Cut a hole into the top of the box, large enough for a child to insert one hand. Place foam packing peanuts (skeleton bones) and wrapped bite-sized candy into the box.

Tell the children that inside the coffin there are skeleton bones and a hidden treasure of candy. They must pull out three pieces of candy from the coffin, without peeking.

Pass the Witch's Broomstick: All the children will be sitting in a circle. As the music starts playing, the children will pass a witch's broomstick (a child-sized broom). When the music stops, whoever is hold-ing the broomstick leaves the circle. This child then goes into the **Spook House** (see below). Continue and the last remaining child is the winner.

Spook House: Cover a table with blankets that touch the floor on all sides of the table. This is the "Spook House." Make it as dark as pos-sible. Fill the house with different Halloween novelties, such as spiders, stickers, pencils, and skeletons. As the child enters the house, give him a flashlight and goody bag. Instruct him to find one each of the different objects. He must exit the house before the next child begins.

The Mixed-Up Witch! Divide the children into teams of six. Each child on the team will need one part of a witch's costume (made from poster board) such as a witch's face, a black dress, a black hat, shoes, a broomstick, or a black cat.

Place a sheet of poster board on the wall for each team. Blindfold the first child on each team and have him walk to the poster board and attach his piece of the witch to it. Blindfold the second child on the team and he will add his piece to the poster board.

Continue until the teams have finished their witches. It will be fun to see how each team has assembled its "Mixed-Up Witch."

Costume Challenge: For this game an adult will need to dress up in a costume, wearing numerous items, such as a whistle, horn, sticker, hat, balloon, or spider.

Have the adult stand in front of the children and let them memorize the costume. Then ask the adult to leave the room and remove one item. Have the adult enter the room and ask the children, "What's Missing?" Let the children call out what they think has been removed.

As an added challenge, move a couple of the objects around and see if they can guess the one that has been omitted.

Wrap a Mummy: Divide the children into pairs. Give each pair a roll of white bathroom tissue. One child will wrap the paper around the other child to make a mummy. When completed, he can "break free" and they will switch roles.

Toss the Candy: Each child will need a personalized grocery bag. Stand the bags side by side with the names hidden from view. The children will stand in front of the bags. Give each child ten pieces of wrapped candy. The children must toss the candy into the bags without knowing the owner of any bags. After all the children have tossed the candy, turn each bag around and distribute to the owner.

Begin with a few pieces of candy in each bag to ensure all children will be receiving a treat.

Bob for Cookies: Hang donuts or butter cookies (with holes in the center) from the ceiling with yarn.

Instruct the children that they must keep their hands behind their backs and try to gobble up the treat using only their mouths.

Sticker Bingo: For each Halloween bingo card, you will need a 6" × 6" square of orange poster board. Using a black marker, divide the cards into nine equal parts, making each a 2" × 2" square. Attach assorted Halloween stickers onto each square varying the designs on each card. Be sure that no two cards are duplicated. Keep one master set of stickers to "call" from.

Using candy corn for bingo chips, play until a card is completely covered for "BINGO." Play several rounds. Use the leftover stickers for bingo prizes.

Add-On Story: Imagination is the big ingredient of this game. As everyone is sitting together in a circle, begin telling a spooky story. After a few sentences, pass the story to the person on your right. He will add to the story and continue to pass it around the circle. It is fun to hear the twists in the plot as your story progresses.

Give the children paper and crayons. Let them draw a scene from the story they have just created.

Broom and Balloon Relay: Divide the children into teams and give each player an inflated balloon. Keep extras on hand in case they are needed. Each team will need a child-sized broom and a large box or laundry basket.

The first person on each team will sweep the balloon with his broom across the party area and into his box. He then runs back to his team and tags the next player to begin sweeping. The first team to complete the race is the winner.

Costume Dress Up Relay: Divide the group into teams. Each team will need a bag of assorted costume accessories, such as a witch's hat, a glove, a large necklace, a clown shoe, a vampire's cape, or a crown. Place each bag at the end of the party area.

The first child on each team will run to the bag and put on everything that is in the bag. When completed, have the child pose for a snapshot. The child must then remove everything and place it back into the bag, and run and tag the next person in line. The first team to finish is the winner.

A Spider's Web: Divide the children into groups with no more than ten to a group. Each group will need one ball of string.

The children will sit in a circle. The first child will take the end of the string and wrap it a couple of times around her finger. She will then tell the joke she has prepared for Halloween night. When finished, she will toss the ball of string (still holding onto the end which is wrapped around her finger) across the circle to another child. Continue to toss the string across the circle until everyone has had a chance to tell a joke. You will have then created a large spider web.

Halloween Word Search: Find the following words in the word search puzzle below. Words may go in any direction—up, down, right, left, or diagonally.

VAMPIRE	SPOOKY	BAT
JACK-O'-LANTERN	GOBLIN	MASKS
BLACK CAT	HAUNTED	GHOST
SKELETON	PUMPKIN	WITCH
TRICK OR TREAT	COSTUME	MUMMY
MIDNIGHT	CALDRON	SPIDER

```
HTASMBFJMHCTIWY
POSVDUWDYACXONT
REDIPSMKNUACFHR
GNSGTLWMLNLOOCI
ADEISHJRYTDKLPC
JACKOLANTERNOWK
SBQTHFNEVDOMQNO
RPABGEHMCZNYIXR
EUOSIJDUNORLPST
RMKOSGMTFGBVAYR
IPLTKVBSUOCPHJE
PKCWSYFOGLBATKA
MIBLACKCATZQFGT
ANXOMIDNIGHTASD
VDESKELETONDLRS
```

Mystery Phrase: Prepare a list of Halloween phrases that the children will decipher. *Examples:*

a) A vampire stopped by for a quick bite.
b) Do witches fly by the seat of their pants?
c) The haunted house was the ghost's home sweet home.
d) The mummy couldn't come to the phone because he was all tied up.

Divide the children into three teams. On a chalkboard, draw a line for each letter of a phrase. Beginning with the first child on team one, ask him to name one letter that he thinks is contained in the phrase. If that letter is in the phrase, write it on all corresponding lines. Ask the second child on the team for another letter. Each correct letter gives that team another turn. If a child asks for a letter that is not in the phrase, the play moves on to the next team.

On each team the children must take turns giving a letter. Teammates may confer but only on the child's turn may he give a letter or solve the phrase. When a team completes the phrase, it will receive one point. Alternate the beginning of each round with a different team.

Costume Awards: This is the portion of the party where everyone wins. Make award ribbons from construction paper. Be certain there are enough awards for every child to receive one. Each award should be in an individual category.

Suggestions:

The Prettiest Costume	The Most Colorful Costume
The Funniest Costume	The Most Realistic Costume
The Scariest Costume	The Longest Tail Award
The Most Beautiful Costume	The Silliest Face Award
The Most Original Costume	The Best Makeup Award

Christmas Party

INVITATIONS

• Fold a piece of green construction paper in half. Cut out a Christmas tree with the left side of the tree on the fold line. Use a hole punch to cut circles from assorted colored construction paper. Glue the circles onto the tree for ornaments. Attach a gold star to the top. Write the invitation information on the inside.

• Place a piece of candy and an invitation inside a small gift box. Wrap the box in Christmas wrapping paper and tie with ribbon. Hand deliver the invitation to each guest.

Suggestion: Ask each guest to bring a wrapped gift to be donated to the needy families in your community.

DECORATIONS

1. To make a table centerpiece (see below) spray paint a small box red. Glue two candy canes to the sides of the box to resemble the blades on a sleigh. Decorate with a bow and fill with candy. To make coordinating party favors see **Sweet Treat** on page 139.

2. "Santa's House" will be used when playing the **Santa Down the Chimney** game (see page 142).

Cut three holes into the top of a large cardboard box (see next page).

Cut one hole in the bottom right side, one hole in the bottom center, and one hole in the bottom left side of the box. Decorate the front of the box to resemble a brick house, and the sides to resemble a Christmas tree and a fireplace with stockings. Decorate three shoe boxes as chimneys and attach around the holes in the top of the box. Attach three pieces of flexible tubing on the inside of the box, connecting each chimney hole with one of the three holes in the box. Accent your house with Christmas lights, and wreaths.

    3. To construct "Santa's Sleigh" you will need the following:

1 large cardboard box	18 antlers, cut from
2 gift wrap rolls	construction paper
red spray paint	helium tank
9 12-inch brown balloons	markers
kite string	

Spray paint the box and cardboard rolls red and attach the rolls to the bottom of the box (see below). Decorate as "Santa's Sleigh."

    Attach two rows of kite string from the sleigh to the wall or ceiling at a 45 degree angle. Inflate the balloons with helium. Draw reindeer faces on the balloons with the markers and attach the antlers. Tie pairs of reindeer to the kite string and place Rudolph at the center top.

    Fill the sleigh with wrapped boxes and a plush Santa toy, or use the sleigh to hold party favors.

REFRESHMENTS

Gift Cake: Bake your favorite cake mix in a 9" × 13" pan. Frost and decorate to resemble a Christmas present, using colored frosting for the ribbon and gift tag.

Rudolph Cupcake: Frost cupcakes with chocolate frosting. Twist two 3-inch pieces of brown pipe cleaner together to form an antler. Insert two antlers into the cupcake. Use two chocolate chips for eyes and a red gumdrop for the nose.

Fudge Cutouts: Melt 3 cups semisweet chocolate chips with 14 ounces sweetened condensed milk. Stir in 1½ teaspoons vanilla. If desired, add 1 cup nuts. Spread evenly into a 9" × 13" pan lined with foil. Refrigerate 2 hours, until firm. Use the foil to lift the fudge from the pan and place it on a cutting board. Peel off the foil and cut into shapes with Christmas cookie cutters. Store tightly covered in a cool, dry place.

Ice Cream Sundaes: Give each child a serving of vanilla ice cream. Offer a variety of toppings and let the children create their own sundae.
Suggested toppings: red and green candy coated chocolate, red and green sprinkles, chocolate chips, nuts, maraschino cherries, bananas, strawberries, marshmallow creme, chocolate syrup, or caramel topping.

Popcorn Snowmen:

20 cups popcorn (2 packages plain microwave popcorn)
½ cup margarine
16 ounces marshmallows
pretzel sticks
red licorice laces
small round candy
gumdrops

Melt margarine and marshmallows together and stir until smooth. Pour marshmallow mixture over popcorn and toss to coat. Immediately grease hands with margarine and shape into popcorn balls. For each snowman, make one 4-inch and one 3-inch ball. Stack the balls together to form the snowman and decorate with pretzel stick arms, candy eyes and nose, red licorice smile, and gumdrop buttons. Makes eight snowmen.

Festive Cookies: Prepare your favorite sugar cookie recipe. Roll to ⅛-inch thickness on a floured surface and cut with Christmas cookie cutters. Bake, frost, and decorate or let the children decorate their own cookie at the party.

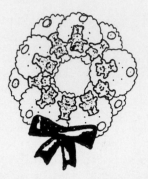

Edible Wreaths: For each wreath, place five round butter crackers in a circle. Frost the bottom side of five additional crackers and place on top, overlapping the first layer. Use frosting to attach candy coated chocolates and bear-shaped cookies onto the wreath. Cut a bow from a red fruit roll-up and attach to the wreath with frosting (see above).

Christmas Banquet: Serve a variety of hot and cold appetizers, banquet style, and let the guests serve themselves.
Suggestions: cocktail wieners in barbecue sauce, pizza rolls, chicken wings, vegetable tray, fruit tray, cheese, salami and crackers.

PARTY FAVORS

Calendar Countdown: For each favor you will need one 11″ × 14″ piece of poster board. Decorate as a calendar, starting with the date of the party through December 25. Cut slits into each day and insert a piece of candy into each slit, with the largest piece on December 25. Give calendars to the children and tell them to countdown to Christmas by eating a piece of candy a day.

Christmas Mouse: Cut the body of a mouse from white felt and the ears from red felt. Cut three slits into the body as shown (see right). Insert the ears through the parallel slits. Glue on moveable eyes. Thread two pieces of black thread for the whiskers. Insert a candy cane through the back slit and the underside of the body between the ears.

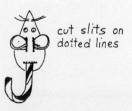

cut slits on dotted lines

Reindeer: Fill two clear plastic cups with candy. Lay a line of tacky glue around the rim of the cups and cover with a circle of brown poster

board. Glue a ⅜-inch wide strip of ribbon around the top and bottom of one cup for the body. Glue the "head" to the body (see right). Cut two antlers from brown poster board or felt and glue to the back of the head. Glue on two moveable eyes and a red pom-pom nose. Glue a bow to the front of the reindeer's neck.

Candy Wreaths: Cut green poster board into a wreath shape. Glue a bow to the top. Fill plastic sandwich bags with candy and tie with ribbons. Attach the bags of candy to the poster board to cover the wreath.

Sweet Treat: For each party favor you will need two miniature candy canes and a small wood chip basket. Cut off the handle of the basket. Glue the candy canes to the sides of the basket and fill the basket with candy. For a coordinating centerpiece see Decorations, page 135.

CRAFTS

Create a Wreath:

30–35 jigsaw puzzle pieces	1 18-inch ribbon
green spray paint	1 6-inch ribbon
green poster board	toothpick
	red acrylic paint

Lay the puzzle pieces flat and spray paint them green. To make a base, cut a 3-inch circle from the poster board. Cut a 2-inch circle from the center.

Glue the puzzle pieces to the base in three tiers, overlapping pieces to cover the base. Make a bow from the 18-inch ribbon and glue to the top of the wreath. Form a loop with the 6-inch ribbon and glue to the back for a hanger. Snip off the point of the toothpick and use it to paint holly berries on the wreath (see below).

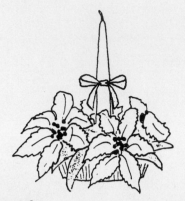

Christmas Candlestick:

plaster of paris	artificial leaves and
1 6-inch pie tin	flowers
1 red 10-inch taper candle	1 red bow

Mix plaster of paris, following instructions on package and fill the pie tin to within ¼ inch of the top. Insert the candle into the center and hold for two minutes to set. Insert the leaves and flowers into the plaster of paris and attach the red bow to the candle (see above).

Snowflake Ornament: Paint four wooden craft sticks white. Attach a ribbon loop to the end of one craft stick to be used as the hanger. Glue the sticks together, overlapping the centers of the sticks, to form a snowflake shape. Decorate with sequins, glitter, or confetti.

Pinecone Ornament: Tie a yarn loop to the top of a pinecone. Pour glue onto a plate. Roll the pinecone into the glue. Holding the pinecone by the loop, place it into a bag filled with metallic confetti. Shake to cover.

Snow Dome:

1 teaspoon of clay	water
1 baby food jar	tiny plastic beads
1 plastic Christmas	1 20-inch ribbon
decoration	

Press the clay flat into the lid of the jar to within ¼ inch of the edge. (Clay in the rim makes it difficult to seal tightly.) Mount your decoration into the clay. Fill the jar with water. Add the beads for "snow." Seal tightly with the lid. Wrap the ribbon around the lid and tie into a bow.

Candy Apple Ornament:
  1 red bead, 1⅝ inch in diameter
  1 candy paper liner, Christmas print
  1 artificial 3-inch candy cane

  Glue the bead inside the candy liner with the hole
at the top. Fill the bead with glue and insert the candy
cane (see right). Hang the candy apple using the candy
cane as the hook.

Holiday Tree: Cut a Christmas tree from green construction
paper. Cut 2″ × 2″ squares of assorted colored tissue paper. Crumple the
tissue squares into small balls. Glue brown balls close together on the
base of the tree for a trunk. Glue assorted colors on the tree for ornaments and a yellow star at the top of the tree.

Reindeer Antlers: For each child, cut a 1″ × 22″ strip of white
poster board. Staple the poster board strip together to form a circle large
enough to fit around a child's head. The children will trace their hands
onto brown construction paper. Cut out the hands and staple them to the
white band for antlers. Paint the child's nose with red acrylic, waterbase
paint to become "Rudolph."

Candy House:
  ½ pint milk carton   assorted decorating treats, such
  construction paper   as candies, cereals, crackers,
  foam tray or plate   bubble gum sticks, etc.

  Prepare the milk carton prior to the party. Open the top of the carton on both sides. Cover each carton with construction paper. Close the
top of the carton to form the roof and glue it together. Glue the carton
to the foam tray.
  The children will choose from the variety of treats and glue them to
the house. An assortment of candy guarantees each child a unique candy
house.

GAMES

Peppermint Toss: Prepare a large, floor-sized mat or poster decorated as a calendar for the month of December. Highlight December 25
on the calendar with bright colors and stickers.
  The children will toss wrapped peppermint candies onto the calendar. If their toss lands on an even number, give them a sticker. If it lands

on an odd number, give them a piece of candy. If their candy lands on December 25, they will win a special grab bag prize.

Santa Down the Chimney: Prepare the "Santa's House" as described under "Decorations" on pages 135–136.

Make a "Santa" to toss by gluing a small felt hat onto a table tennis ball. Draw on Santa's face with a marker.

Each child will toss the Santa into the chimneys. Santa will fall through the house and land in one of three places. The goal is to send Santa down the chimney chute which lands at the fireplace to win a prize. Label the other exits with signs saying "Try Again" or offer small trinkets at those exits.

Build a Snowman Relay: For each team you will need the following items:

3 cardboard boxes, decreasing in size	2 paper eyes
2 small tree branches	1 paper nose
2 mittens	1 paper mouth
1 scarf	1 paper pipe
1 hat	double-stick tape

Paint the cardboard boxes white or cover them with white paper to be used as the body of the snowman. Cut slits in the middle-sized box for inserting the branches. Place double-stick tape on the back of the facial features and pipe.

Each team must build its snowman and add all the accessories before the other teams finish. To begin, the first person on each team will run and stack the middle-sized box on top of the largest box. He runs back and tags his teammate who will run and add the head of the snowman. The next player will add one accessory. The first team to complete its snowman is the winner.

Stocking-Go-Round: Seat the children in a circle. When the music starts, pass a Christmas stocking filled with party favor bags around the circle. When the music is stopped, the child holding the stocking removes one party favor bag and leaves the circle. He will then play the **Santa's Bag** game (see below). Continue until each child is given a party favor bag.

Santa's Bag: This is a guessing game that requires the children to use their senses of touch and memory. Fill a large bag with a variety of objects which will be identified only by feeling them. Blindfold the child and he will pick something from "Santa's Bag." He must guess what he is holding without peeking.

Candy Cane Competition: Divide the children into pairs. For each pair you will need the following:

1 small roll of red crepe paper
1 small roll of white crepe paper
a stand made by mounting a wrapping paper roll into a shoebox

Give one child the red and the other child the white crepe paper. When told to go, each child begins to wrap his streamers around the tube to make a candy cane. The first pair to complete a candy cane is the winner.

Sing and Shout "Merry Christmas!" Sing the following song to the tune of "The Twelve Days of Christmas." Create motions to do for each of Santa's sayings.

On the first day of Christmas Santa said to me,
"Loudly shout Merry Christmas!"
On the second day of Christmas Santa said to me,
"Blink like the lights,
and loudly shout Merry Christmas!"

Continue as listed below:

1st day — "loudly shout Merry Christmas!"
2nd day — "blink like the lights"
3rd day — "prance like a reindeer"
4th day — "melt like a snowman"
5th day — "shout HO—HO—HO"
6th day — "fly like an angel"
7th day — "stand like a candy cane"
8th day — "walk like a soldier"
9th day — "scowl like the Grinch"
10th day — "choo-choo like a train"
11th day — "drum like a drummer"
12th day — "roll like a snowball"

Catch the Snowball: Divide the children into groups of four to five. Each group needs one small bucket and three "snowballs" (white pom-poms).

One child from each group will sit in a chair approximately six feet from her team and will hold the bucket on her head. The other players will take turns throwing the three snowballs at the child who will be trying to catch them in the bucket. Take turns catching the snowballs. The team that catches the most snowballs is the winner.

The Human Tree: Purchase green nylon netting and cut a circle in the center large enough to slip over a head. Ask a volunteer to put on the netting. Give the children an assortment of decorations and let them decorate "The Human Tree." Glue a star on a headband to be used as the tree topper.

Exchange a Gift: Ask each child attending the party to bring a wrapped gift for someone of the same sex and label the gift tag "For Girl, from Amy" or "For Boy, from Eric." Set a spending limit.

When the children arrive at the party, place the girls' and boys' gifts separately under the tree.

Select a Christmas story to read to the group. Give each child a piece of paper with a different word written on it (which has been selected from the story).

Read the story out loud. When the children hear their word during the story, they will select a present from under the tree. Instruct the children not to open their gifts until the story is ended. This way they can enjoy the story without interruption and will open the gifts together.

Name That Tune: Collect a variety of Christmas music. Give each child a pencil and an answer sheet. Play only a few notes from each song and the children will write down what song they think is being played. The person with the most correct answers wins.

"What Am I?" Divide the children into teams. One child on each team is given a card. He will try to get his teammates to guess the word written on that card. However, he may not use the clue words on the card. The team to correctly solve the most cards during a specific amount of time is the winner.

Example:

(the answer your teammates must say)	Candy Cane
(clue words not allowed to give)	Red
	White
	Sweet

Secret Message: Photocopy one "Secret Message," as illustrated on page 145, for each child. Cut it into a tree shape and glue onto construction paper. After it has dried, fold the paper in half and punch a hole into the top. Attach a pencil with contrasting ribbon or yarn through the hole. Personalize and decorate the cover as desired.

Instruct the children that this is a secret message and each object represents a letter. They must use the key at the bottom to break the message.

Solution: A Merry Christmas to All and to All a Fun Vacation.

Follow the Star: Divide the children into groups of three to four. Remind them how the Wise Men followed the star to find baby Jesus. Their goal also, is to follow the stars.

Cut four or five construction paper stars for each team. To begin the "journey," each group receives one star. On that star is written a clue that will lead them to the next star. *Example:* "Travel to a place where you get a sharp point" (the pencil sharpener). There they will find another star with another clue. Each group should have individual clues and will follow its own directions.

The game continues until they reach the final star, which has a picture of baby Jesus on it. This would be a fun place to put star-shaped sugar cookies, or give each child a glitter covered star badge made from poster board.

Away in a Manger: Prior to the party, make a cradle for baby Jesus. This can be made from an oatmeal box, cut as shown on the next page.

A cradle for "Away in a Manger" game.

Give each child several 3-inch pieces of yellow yarn. Begin singing the song "Away in a Manger." As you are singing, have each child place his yarn in the cradle to prepare it for Jesus. At the end of the song, Jesus will have a soft bed of "straw" in His manger. After the cradle is ready, the teacher (or the child hosting the party) can place a small doll, wrapped in a white cloth, into the bed.

Valentine's Day Party

INVITATIONS

Indicate on the invitation if the children will be exchanging valentine cards amongst themselves. Be sure to let each child know how many children will be attending and to bring a valentine for every child.

- Fold one piece of construction paper in half. Trace, and cut a bear pattern, making sure the heart is on the fold of your paper (see below). Draw the bear's face and write the party information on the inside of the heart.

- Cut five hearts from construction paper. Glue them together on your invitation to make a caterpillar (see below). Draw the legs and facial features and write all necessary information on the hearts.

● Cut two hearts, one slightly larger than the other, from construction paper. Glue the smaller heart onto the larger one (see below). Draw a lion's facial features and a mane. Cut a larger heart for the body. Glue the head onto the point of this heart. Cut and glue a heart onto the end of a tail and attach it to the body. Write on the body, "I'd be 'lion' if I said I didn't want you to come to my party."

DECORATIONS

1. Decorate your table with a lollipop centerpiece using the following:

heart lollipops (1 per child)	1 4-inch Styrofoam ball, cut in half
20 2" × 12" strips of red tissue paper	1 9-inch red poster board circle
20 2" × 12" strips of white tissue paper	straight pins

Glue the flat edge of the ball to the center of the poster board circle. Insert the lollipops into the ball. Fanfold the tissue paper and secure between the lollipops with the pins (see below).

2. Hang the **Heart to Heart** party favors (see page 150) with red and white yarn.

3. Make Cupid's arrows from red construction paper. Write each guest's name on an arrow. Decorate the wall with a large Cupid cutout and the personalized arrows.

4. Fill red and white heart-shaped balloons with helium. Tie with coordinated ribbon to the back of each child's chair.

REFRESHMENTS

Valentine Sweetheart Cake: Prepare a cake mix and bake in heart-shaped cake pans. Frost with vanilla frosting and decorate with conversation hearts or red candy-coated chocolate.

Eat Your Heart Out!
2 6-ounce packages red gelatin
3 cups boiling water

Stir water into the gelatin to dissolve completely. Pour into a 9" x 13" pan. Chill at least four hours. Cut into heart shapes with a cookie cutter.

Chocolate Ice Cream Cups:
1 6-ounce package semisweet chocolate chips
8 foil baking cups

8 scoops vanilla ice cream
red sprinkles

Melt chocolate chips in a double boiler over hot, but not boiling water. Remove from heat. Stir until smooth. Line a muffin pan with foil baking cups. With the back of a spoon, spread one heaping teaspoon of chocolate into each foil cup, covering the sides and bottom. Be sure to completely cover the surface of the cup. Refrigerate overnight. Before serving, peel the foil from the chocolate cups. Fill each cup with a scoop of vanilla ice cream. Top with red sprinkles. Serve immediately or freeze until ready to serve. Makes eight individual cups.

Heart-Shaped Treats: Melt ¼ cup margarine and 10 ounces of marshmallows together until smooth. Stir in 6 cups of toasted rice cereal. Press the mixture firmly into a greased 9" x 13" pan. Cut into heart shapes and top each heart with a chocolate candy.

Ice Cream Sodas: Place one scoop of vanilla ice cream into a clear, plastic cup. Pour strawberry or cream soda into each cup and serve with a spoon and a straw.

Honey Hearts:
> ½ cup mashed banana
> ½ cup peanut butter
> 1 tablespoon honey

Combine the above ingredients. Cut 48 slices of white bread with a 4-inch heart cookie cutter. Spread two teaspoons of the peanut butter mixture on 24 slices of the bread. Top with remaining bread cutouts.

PARTY FAVORS

Heart to Heart: Glue a white heart doily to a red poster board heart. Cut 1-inch slits throughout the heart. Personalize the heart and insert candy into each slit.

Heart Carts: Glue a red heart, cut from construction paper, onto a nut cup. Bend two pipe cleaners into a cane shape and glue to the back of the cup for the cart handles. Glue two hard candy circles onto each side for wheels. Fill with candy treats (see illustration A below).

A   B

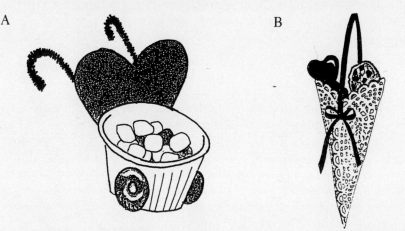

Valentine Roll-Ups: Cut one piece of pink or red construction paper slightly smaller than a doily and glue it to the doily. Roll the doily into a cone shape and glue the ends. Glue the ends of one 8-inch piece of ribbon onto each side of the cone. Decorate with a bow. Fill with candy and treats (see illustration B above).

Sweetheart Surprise: Fill a red plastic cup with valentine treats. Enclose the cup in red plastic film wrap and secure with red yarn.

Cupid's Arrow: Use a white tissue paper holder for the body of the arrow. If desired, the children may decorate these with stickers or red markers. From red construction paper, cut two feathers and two arrows. Glue the arrows and feathers onto the roll as shown above. Fill with candy. Cut a 2-inch circle from poster board and glue over the end of the tube.

CRAFTS

Valentine Necklace:

colored straws cut into 1-inch lengths	small hearts cut from construction paper
1 30-inch piece of yarn	1 bobby pin

Punch a hole into the center of each heart. Thread the yarn into the bobby pin to act as a needle. String hearts and straws onto the yarn, alternating one heart, one straw, etc. Tie the ends together.

Red Sidewalk Chalk:

½ cup plaster of paris	¼ cup water
⅛ cup red powdered tempera paint	sealable plastic bag

Mix together plaster of paris and paint powder and place the mixture into the bag containing ¼ cup water. Knead until it is the consistency of dough. Secure the bag with tape to a table so it is hanging off the table. The mixture should now resemble a log at the bottom of the bag. Allow 30 minutes to dry.

Valentine Mailbox: Cover a shoe box with white construction paper. Cut a slit in the top to insert valentine cards. Cut out hearts from red and pink construction paper varying in sizes. The children can decorate the mailboxes using the hearts, stickers, markers, doilies, and ribbons. After everyone has finished, deliver the valentine cards to the mailboxes.

U.S. Mail Truck: Seal to close a 9½″ × 12½″ white mailing envelope. Cut out a 4″ × 4″ square from the top corner. Glue on two black circles at the bottom for the tires. Cut a ½″ × 12″ strip from blue construction paper and glue it across the envelope (see above). Let the children design their own mail truck and have them deliver their valentines.

My Autograph Book: The children can create their own autograph book. Each classmate can write her name and a short phrase on the page of her choice.

Fold one piece of red construction paper in half and decorate for the cover. For the pages, fold two pieces of white paper in half, and insert them inside of the cover. Punch two holes on the left side of the book, insert yarn, and tie into a bow. Attach a valentine pencil or marker to the yarn. At the top of each page write headings, such as the following: My Playmates, My Scouting Buddies, My Soccer Buddies, My Baseball Buddies, My Recess Friends, My Dancing Partners, My Hopscotch Friends, My Kickball Team, My Fellow Band Members, My Favorite Teachers.

Party Place Mats:

| 1 9″ × 12″ red construction paper | 1 9″ × 12″ white construction paper |
| 18 red heart stickers | clear Contact paper |

Fold the red construction paper in half. Make five cuts, 1½ inches apart, up from the folded line, leaving a 1-inch border at the top. Cut six, 1½-inch wide strips from the white paper. Unfold the red construction paper and weave the white strips in and out forming red and white squares (see next page). On each white square place a heart sticker. Cover

the front and back with the Contact paper, leaving a 1-inch border around the place mat.

Sweet Hearts: Cut one heart from red construction paper. Cut a piece of clear Contact paper slightly larger than the construction paper heart. Place the Contact paper on top, and trim to the same size as the paper heart. Cut the same size heart shape from heavy clear plastic. Place on top of the first heart and punch holes, evenly spaced, all around the heart. Cut a 36-inch piece of yarn. Starting at the top of the heart, "sew" around the heart, leaving about eight inches of yarn at the start to tie the bow. Sew until you are approximately three inches from where you started. Fill the heart with valentine candy. Sew the heart closed. Tie the ends of the yarn together into a bow (see below).

GAMES

Valentine Card Exchange: The children will sit in a circle holding a personalized container and the valentine cards they will be distributing. At the sound of a clap, each child will pass his container to the right. Everyone will place one card into the container he is holding. Clap again and continue passing to the right and distributing cards.

After several passes, randomly select a name. The person's name that has been picked and the child who is holding that person's container will each receive a prize. Continue passing until all names have been picked.

Note: Notify the teacher that the cards will be exchanged at the Valentine party. Inform each child that the envelopes are not to be personalized.

Hoop the Candy: Divide the children into groups. Give each group two hoops (these can be embroidery hoops or cut from a plastic lid). Spread wrapped candy around the floor approximately five feet from where each group is standing. Give each child several chances to toss the hoop onto the candy. The child will keep the candy that is inside of the hoop.

Follow Your Heart Relay: Cut a heart from poster board for each team member. Print instructions for different activities on each heart, such as the following:

a) mimic Cupid's shooting arrows
b) run backwards
c) skip
d) take baby steps
e) do logrolls
f) leap like a ballerina

Divide the children into teams. The first player on each team will run to the cards, read the top card, and follow the directions back to his team. The game continues until each person has had a turn. The first team to have all players complete their activity wins.

Find My Name: Make each child a nameplate by cutting poster board into a 6¼" × 12" rectangle. Fold the long edge up ¼ inch. Fold into thirds and glue to form a triangle (see next page).

Cut out individual letters from construction paper which spell the name of every child at the party. Have materials on hand to make additional letters if needed.

Mix up the letters and evenly distribute them to each child. The children will now approach each other asking for the letters they need to spell their name. *Example:* Eric needs to spell E-R-I-C. David has an E that he does not need. Eric will approach David and say, "David, can I

have your E?" David then hands Eric the E. Eric will go to Amy and say, "Amy, can I have your R?" The game continues until all of the children have completed their name. They will now glue their letters onto the nameplate and decorate as desired.

Heart Throb: Glue an assortment of pictures of teen idols to a poster board and attach to the wall. Each child will shoot at this poster using Cupid's bow and arrow (a toy bow shooting soft-tipped arrows). The teen idol struck by Cupid's arrow will become that child's true love.

Who's Hiding the Heart? Divide the children into groups of ten or less, and seat everyone in a circle. One player is "it" and sits inside the circle. Everyone will hold on to a string that is long enough to go around the entire circle. Thread a small heart cutout onto the string.

As the music starts, each player will hold the string with both hands and move her hands along the string. The heart is hidden in someone's hand and is being passed from hand to hand. When the music stops "it" must try to guess who is hiding the heart. The game continues until everyone has had a turn to hide the heart and to be "it."

Plate Full of Hearts: Divide the group into teams. Place one plate six feet away from each team. The first child on each team will try to toss five candy hearts onto the plate. Leave the hearts which have landed on the plate, and the second player will toss his five hearts. After everyone has had a turn, count the number of hearts on the plate. The team with the most hearts on the plate wins.

Human Valentines: Glue valentines onto spring-type clothespins. Each team will need ten clothespins.

Divide the children into teams and have them stand in rows. On the count of three, the first person in each row will run to the valentines and clip them onto himself. He will then race back to his teammates and remove all the clothespins. The second child then clips the valentines on, runs to where the valentines originally were located and takes them off. He then runs back to his teammates and tags the third child in line. If any valentines fall off while the children are moving from place to place, they must stop and clip them back onto their clothes. The first team to finish is the winner.

Guess How Many: Fill a small plastic bag for each child with candy and tie with decorative ribbon. Make one larger bag of candy to be used as the jackpot bag for the winner. Place all the bags in a clear jar. Each child will try to guess the total amount of candy in the jar. The child closest to the correct amount will win the jackpot bag. Give the rest of the bags to the children for their goody bags.

Pass the Party Favor Bag: Divide the children into groups of six. Each child will have one lunch bag containing six of one object, such as the following:

6 suckers	6 stickers
6 erasers	6 markers
6 pencils	6 heart-shaped balloons

At the start of the music, all the children will randomly trade bags with each other as fast as they can. When the music stops, each child will remove one prize from the bag he is holding. Again, start the music and the trading continues. Do not take a prize if it is a duplicate. Keep playing and trading until everyone has one of each prize. As bags are emptied, eliminate them from the circle.

Debate and Decide: Divide the children into teams of four or five. Each team will need a pencil and answer sheet. (Paper cut into heart shapes will fit the theme.) Number the answer sheets from one to four.

Pick a letter of the alphabet and ask four questions whose answers must begin with the letter picked. The team will decide together on an answer and write it down. When the teams have finished the four questions, each team will announce its answers. The goal is to have an answer not given by another team. To score a point, the answer has to start with the correct letter and not be duplicated by another team. Example:

Letter R—question and (possible answers)
a) things you do at school (recess, run, relays, read)
b) cartoon character (Roadrunner, Raphael, Roger Rabbit)
c) name an animal (rhino, rabbit, rat, raccoon, robin)
d) something you find in your lunch box (raisins, Ruffles, rotten apple, root beer)

Letter C—questions and (possible answers)
a) a gift from your sweetheart on Valentine's Day (chocolate, card, candy)

b) a sweetheart's name (Carol, Cindy, Connie, Chris, Carl, Chip)
c) something you do at a party (crafts, cake, centerpiece, come)
d) a food served at a party (candy, chips, carrots, chocolate)

If desired, use the **Heart to Heart** party favor (see page 150) to keep score. Each child will receive one piece of candy in her scoreboard for each correct answer from her team.

"Who Am I?" You will need one blank sticker for each child. On each sticker write one name from a famous couple, such as the following: Mickey Mouse/Minnie Mouse, Donald Duck/Daisy Duck, Barbie/Ken, Kermit the Frog/Miss Piggy, Robin Hood/Maid Marion, Santa Claus/Mrs. Claus, Popeye/Olive Oyl, Fred Flintstone/Wilma Flintstone, Barney Rubble/Betty Rubble, Bam Bam/Pebbles, George Jetson/Jane Jetson, Porky Pig/Petunia Pig, Cinderella/Prince Charming, Ariel/Prince Eric, Belle/Beast.

Place a sticker on the back of each player without him seeing it. The children will then try to guess who they are by asking each other questions, such as "Am I a cartoon character?"; "Am I a girl?"; "Am I on TV?"; "Am I a child?" The only answer a child is allowed to give is "yes" or "no."

Human Bingo: Prepare heart-shaped bingo cards. Draw nine squares on the cards. In each square write phrases, making sure no two bingo cards are the same.

Suggested phrases:
is wearing red
made a valentine card for someone
is the oldest child in the family
has curly hair
has a red lunch box
owns a dog
likes strawberry ice cream
has gone horseback riding
likes to play basketball

Every child will take his bingo card around to the class. When he finds someone fitting the description in a square, he will write that person's name in that square. When he has filled his whole card with names, he has won the game.

Crossword Puzzle: Photocopy one crossword puzzle for each child. Attach a pencil, with yarn, to each puzzle and distribute to the party guests (see next page).

Across

    1) A weapon shot from a bow
    2) A peck
    3) To court with flowers and candy
    4) A color on Valentine's Day
    5) A body organ
    6) Words and music put together
    7) A color you turn when you blush
    8) Sweetheart holiday
    9) Sweets for your sweetheart
    10) Something you mail

Down

    9) Someone who shoots an arrow
    10) Darling
    11) Shoots arrows
    12) Valentine's Day date
    13) _____ are red
    14) What Valentine's Day is all about
    15) A Valentine's Day celebration

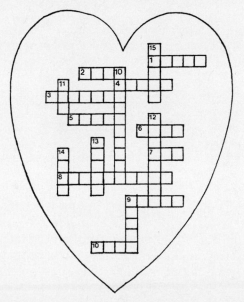

Answers:
Across: 1. arrow; 2. kiss; 3. romance; 4. white; 5. heart; 6. song; 7. red;
8. Valentine's; 9. candy; 10. card. Down: 9. Cupid; 10. sweetheart; 11. bow;
12. fourteen; 13. roses; 14. love; 15. party

Easter Party

INVITATIONS

- Cut yellow construction paper into the shape of a chick. Write all necessary party information on the chick and place it inside a plastic egg. Hand deliver the invitation to your guests.
- Fold a piece of construction paper in half and cut a bunny shape on the fold line. Draw a bunny face on each invitation. On the outside of the invitation write "Hop on Over to My Party!" Write the party information on the inside.
- Cut two Easter baskets from construction paper. Glue along the outside edges, leaving the center of the basket open. Cut Easter eggs from assorted colored construction paper. Write the party information on the eggs. Place the eggs inside the basket.

DECORATIONS

1. Make an Easter train for the table centerpiece (see below). If desired, you may make one train car for each child to take home. Purchase small individual-sized wicker baskets from your local craft store. Decorate with lace around the outer edge on each basket. Glue four, 2-inch wooden wheels onto each basket. Use 6-inch pieces of ribbon to connect the train cars. Fill with Easter grass and place a small bunny into each car.

2. Fill 12-inch balloons with helium. Draw bunny faces on the balloons. Cut construction paper ears and attach to the balloons. Tie a bunny balloon onto each guest's chair.

REFRESHMENTS

Easter Bunny Cake: Prepare a cake mix and bake in two 9-inch round pans. Freeze one layer for later use. Let the cake cool and then cut in half to make two semicircles. Frost the top of one semicircle and layer them together. Stand the pieces upright on the cut edge on your serving tray. Cut a notch about 1/3 of the way up on one side of the body to form the head, and use the notched piece for the tail (see below). Frost the entire cake, rounding the body on the sides. Sprinkle with one cup of coconut. Cut ears from pink construction paper and press into the top. Use jelly beans for eyes and nose. Shake one cup coconut with three drops of green food coloring in a plastic bag until evenly tinted. Place the green coconut around the bunny and add jelly beans.

If desired, substitute white chocolate curls for coconut. Scrape a white chocolate bar with a vegetable parer to form curls.

Easter Basket Cupcakes: Bake cupcakes and frost with vanilla frosting. Bend a 6-inch pipe cleaner to form the basket handle and insert it into the top of the cupcake. Place one cup of coconut and three drops of green food coloring in a bag and shake until evenly colored. Sprinkle the coconut onto the cupcake and add small jelly beans for Easter eggs.

Cookie Bunnies: For each bunny, frost a large, round sugar cookie with vanilla frosting. Use two chocolate chips for eyes, a jelly bean for the nose, and red, string licorice for whiskers. Cut one oval cookie in half and place at the top of the bunny for the ears.

Bunny Munchies: Serve the children "bunny food." Glue half of a plastic Easter egg on a small paper plate with a hot-melt glue gun. Fill the egg with vegetable dip or salad dressing. Serve with a variety of fresh vegetables.

Crispy Easter Baskets:

⅓ cup light corn syrup	3 cups crispy rice cereal
½ cup brown sugar	1 cup shredded coconut (optional)
¾ cup peanut butter	36 jelly beans
1 teaspoon vanilla	12 6-inch pipe cleaners

Bring the corn syrup, brown sugar, peanut butter and vanilla to a boil. Remove from heat. Stir in cereal and coconut. Let cool until touchable. Shape into balls the size of a small orange and place into a muffin tin. Indent the middle of the rice mixture with your thumb and press around the sides of the tin to form a basket. Add three small jelly beans for eggs. Insert a pipe cleaner into the sides to make the basket handle. Makes 12 baskets.

Chick Nuggets: Purchase enough chicken nuggets for each child to receive approximately four nuggets. Prepare according to directions on package. Serve with catsup, honey, or sweet-and-sour sauce.

PARTY FAVORS

Funny Bunny: Draw a bunny face on the back of a white plastic spoon. Glue pink construction paper ears to the front of the spoon. Attach a sucker to the spoon with ribbon and tie into a bow.

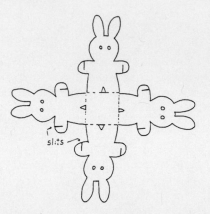

Bunny Egg Holders: Cut a bunny pattern from colored construction paper (see above). Make eyes with a small hole punch. Cut slits as shown. Fold up on the dotted lines and interlock the arms. Fill with Easter grass and a filled, plastic egg.

Bunny Bags: Purchase one white lunch bag for each child. Design bunny faces as shown below, using pink felt for the cheeks and ears, moveable eyes, a pom-pom for the nose, and black pipe cleaners for whiskers. Outline the teeth with a black marker. Fill with treats.

A bunny puppet can be made by inverting the bunny on the bag.

Egg-citing Bunnies:

6-inch pipe cleaner
1 large plastic Easter egg
2 fabric ears, stiffened
   with fabric softener
1 small ribbon bow

2 moveable eyes
fine point permanent marker
1 small pom-pom
candy

Bend the pipe cleaner into a heart shape and glue to the bottom of the egg (see above). Fold the ears ½ inch from the bottom and glue to the front of the egg. Attach the bow in the middle of the ears with a hot-melt glue gun. Glue on the two eyes and draw the facial features. Glue the pom-pom on the back for the tail. Fill the egg with candy.

Washcloth Bunnies:

1 white washcloth
2 rubber bands
8-inch piece of ribbon
2 moveable eyes
1 small pink pom-pom

black marker
1 cotton ball
1 small plastic egg filled
    with treats

a) Lay the washcloth flat and tightly roll one corner towards the center (see illustration A).
b) Roll the opposite corner toward the center.
c) For the body of the bunny, fold the washcloth in half and tie with one rubber band three inches above the fold (see illustration B).
d) Wrap the second rubber band 1½ inches above the first rubber band to form the head.
e) Tie ribbon around the neck of the bunny to hide the rubber band.
f) Glue eyes onto the bunny (see illustration C).
g) Glue on the pom-pom for the nose.
h) Draw a bunny mouth and whiskers with the marker.
i) Glue the cotton ball onto the back for the tail.
j) Insert the egg into the opening of the tummy.

A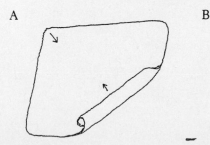

B

C

CRAFTS

Dye Easter Eggs: This is an all time favorite for children no matter what age. We recommend dividing into groups, and letting each child dye one or two eggs. Only use dyes made with food coloring or a nontoxic base.

Fluffy Bunnies: Photocopy a large Easter bunny from a coloring book. Give the children white cotton balls to glue onto the body of the bunny, and pink cotton balls for the ears and nose. Tear one blue cotton ball in half and glue on for the eyes.

Easter Bonnets: Purchase painter hats, straw hats, or make hats (see **Fanciful Hats** pages 59–60) for each child. Let the children decorate their hats with markers, crayons, or paints. If desired, you may wish to stencil baskets, bunnies or eggs on the hats and let the children color in the designs. Offer ornamentations, such as Easter grass, small chicks, eggs, or bunnies to glue onto the hats.

Be a Bunny: Cut a 1″ × 22″ strip from poster board and staple to form a circle. Cut two bunny ears from white poster board and two ears, slightly smaller, from pink construction paper. Glue the pink ears to the white ears and staple them to the circle.

Paint the children's noses pink, with waterbase paint, and draw whiskers on their cheeks with an eyebrow pencil. Now the "bunnies" are ready for the Easter party.

Bunny Baskets: Cut an empty gallon milk jug into the shape of a bunny as shown below. Glue on two large moveable eyes, a pink pom-pom for the nose, two white cotton balls for cheeks, and pink cotton balls for ears. Glue pipe cleaners on each side of the face for whiskers. Decorate the baskets with markers. Tie a bow tie and glue to the neck.

cut on line

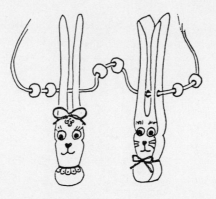

Bunny Necklace:

2 flat-head clothespins	fine point marker
4 small moveable eyes	24-inch ribbon
yarn	6 beads

a) Drill holes through the clothespins, as illustrated above.
b) Glue on the eyes.
c) Tie a bow with yarn at the top of the head to make a girl bunny and a bow tie around the neck to make a boy bunny.
d) Draw on facial features with the marker adding eyelashes and a lace collar on the girl.
e) String the beads and clothespins onto the ribbon alternating two beads, one clothespin, two beads, one clothespin and two beads. Tie the two ends into a knot.

Cross Pins:

2 3-inch pieces of 3mm	4 4mm facet beads
pipe cleaner	1 small decorative flower
19 12mm paddle wheel beads	1 bar pin

Twist the pipe cleaners together into the shape of a cross. Place seven paddle wheels onto the bottom of the cross and four paddle wheels onto the top and sides. Press the wheels together. Glue the facet beads onto the ends and trim any remaining pipe cleaner. Glue the flower in the center of the cross and the bar pin onto the back (see below).

Bunny Visors:

white poster board
pink construction paper
1 plastic sun visor
2 large moveable eyes

1 small pink pom-pom
4 6-inch black pipe cleaners
marker
17-inch ribbon

Cut ears from the white poster board and slightly smaller ears from the pink construction paper. Glue them together. Glue the ears onto the visor. Glue on the eyes, the pom-pom for the nose, and the pipe cleaners for whiskers. Draw on a mouth. Glue the ribbon across the band of the visor (see above).

GAMES

Scrambled Eggs: Cut poster board into egg shapes and decorate in different colors and patterns. Cut each egg in half in a jagged pattern to form two puzzle pieces.

Randomly distribute one egg half to each child. The children will race to find the person who has the other half of their egg.

These partners can be used as teams for future games, such as **Pull the Bunny Tail** (see below). To group the children into larger teams, cut the eggs into numerous puzzle pieces.

Pull the Bunny Tail: Make a bunny tail by wrapping yarn around a 3-inch piece of cardboard 25 times. Slip it off the cardboard and tie in half using a 12-inch piece of yarn. Cut the loops on each end.

Tape one tail onto the back of each child. Divide into partners and have them face each other. On the signal "One, two, three, Bunny!" each child will try to grab her partner's tail and pull it off, while trying to keep her own tail from being grabbed.

Easter Scramble: Divide the children into teams of four to five per team. Scramble Easter words, made from plastic magnetic letters, onto a cookie sheet and give one sheet to each team. The first team to correctly arrange its word wins that round. Be prepared to put the next assortment of letters onto the sheets and begin again.

Eggs in a Basket: Each child will need one straw and one piece of colored tissue paper cut into the shape of an egg. Have the children practice holding the egg to the bottom of the straw by inhaling through the straw. Place one Easter basket at the end of the room for each team.

Divide the group into teams. The first player on each team inhales through the straw and carries his egg across the party area to be put into the basket. He will run back and tag the second child on his team. That child will do the same with his egg. The game continues until one team has placed all its eggs into the basket.

"Happy Easter" Message: Divide the group into teams of four or five. Prepare a scoreboard for each team by drawing a row of 11 squares on a poster board. The object is to spell out "Happy Easter" in the squares. You will need 11 plastic eggs for each team. Write the letters of "Happy Easter" on individual stickers. Place one sticker in each egg and hide them around the room.

To begin the game, the first person on each team will find a hidden egg, bring it back to his scoreboard, and remove the letter that is inside the egg. He will place that letter in the appropriate square on the scoreboard. The next child on the team will do the same. If he picks an egg with a letter already on the scoreboard, he must return the egg to the same spot he found it. The first team to complete its message wins the game.

The Bunny Leap: Divide the children into teams. Stand each team in a line with the children approximately two feet apart. The children will squat low to the ground. Instruct the children that they are pretending to be the Easter Bunny and they must hop over their teammates (similar to Leap Frog). Give the last child in each line a plastic egg. He will carry the egg and hop over each teammate until he is at the front of the row. He will then pass the egg between his legs to the child behind him, and all the players will continue to pass the egg back until it is in the hands of the last player in the row. This player will then begin hopping forward. Play continues until each person has hopped over all the other players. The children should then be in their original order. The first team to finish is the winner.

Create a Bunny: Divide the children into teams. Give each team one sheet of poster board, markers, and one die. Each number on the die represents a part of the bunny they will be drawing.

1 = head	4 = mouth
2 = one ear	5 = one eye
3 = nose	6 = one whisker

Place the children in a circle and pass the die around. The first child to roll a one will draw the head onto the poster board. Pass the die and after each roll the child will draw one bunny part. If that part is already completed, the turn passes on. Continue rolling and drawing until the bunny is complete with one head, two ears, one nose, one mouth, two eyes, and six whiskers. The first team to complete its bunny wins. After all teams have completed their bunnies, display for everyone to see.

Colored Eggs: Divide the children into six teams. Each child will have one colored, plastic egg, matching his teammates. For instance, for 30 children you will need five yellow, five orange, five purple, five pink, five green and five blue eggs. You will also need one egg of each color to be put into a basket.

The children will hide their egg behind their back to keep its color a secret. Pick one color to be "it" (the wolves). All other children are the bunnies who are standing on the baseline facing the wolves.

One of the wolves randomly picks a colored egg from the basket. *Example:* If the wolf picks a blue egg, all the wolves and bunnies then say:

wolves: "Knock, knock"
bunnies: "Who's there?"
wolves: "Big bad wolf"
bunnies: "What do you want?"
wolves: "Colored eggs"
bunnies: "What color?"
wolves: "Blue!"

All the bunnies whose secret color is blue run from base and are chased by the wolves. The object is to try to return to the base without being caught. The blue bunnies will then become the next wolves.

Decorate My Egg: Cut one large egg from poster board for each child. This will be his scoreboard. From construction paper, cut one blue circle, one green square, one pink heart, and one yellow triangle for each child. Draw these shapes with coordinating markers on each scoreboard. Place the cutouts of each shape into their own paper bag.

The game begins with everyone sitting in a circle. As music starts playing, the children will pass the four bags around the circle. When the music stops, the players holding a bag remove a shape and place it on their scoreboard. The game continues until everyone has one of each shape.

Bunny Hop: Record the "Bunny Hop" song onto a cassette approximately three times in succession. Stand the children in a line, holding the waist of the child in front of them. Teach the children the dance to go along with the song:
Put your right foot forward (two right foot kicks)
Put your left foot out (two left foot kicks)
Do (one hop forward)
the bunny hop (one hop backward)
hop, hop, hop (three hops forward)

Eggs-press the Message: Place a basket filled with plastic eggs on the floor. All the children should sit in a circle around the basket. In each egg, place a written message. Take turns selecting an egg from the basket and following the directions on the message inside.
Suggested messages:

a) Hop like a bunny around the circle.
b) Draw an Easter basket on the chalkboard.
c) Hide an egg in a special place.
d) Eat a jelly bean.
e) Name something you find in your Easter basket.
f) Tell what you do on Easter morning.
g) Draw a decorated Easter egg.

Older children may enjoy doing this game like charades. They will act out what is written on the message, such as the following:

a) Dye an Easter egg.
b) Peel a hard boiled egg.
c) Go to church.
d) Be the Easter Bunny hiding Easter eggs.
e) Eat an Easter egg.
f) Have your Easter picture taken.
g) Eat a chocolate bunny.

Easter Code: In this game, you will need to break the Easter Bunny's secret code and find his hidden treasure.
Divide the children into groups. Assign each team a color for its team name and give each group a treasure map. On the map is a list of clues where the Easter Bunny has hidden his eggs. Each team will need

to decipher the clues to find the special hiding spots. List the same clues on each, but in a different order, to prevent all of the teams from going to the same place at the same time.

In each location, hide a colored paper egg for each team that corresponds to their team's name. The first team to decipher the secret code and to collect all its eggs is the winner.

Suggested clues:

a) Midnight two-by-four (the blackboard)
b) Enter and exit here (the door)
c) A place to keep your books (bookcase)
d) This makes mistakes disappear (eraser)
e) Where you stick a thumbtack (bulletin board)
f) Captain Hook's greatest fear (clock)
g) Oscar's home (trash can)
h) Where you would go to get a point (pencil sharpener)
i) This one is bigger than the other 30 in the classroom (teacher's desk)

Pass an Egg: Everyone sits in a circle. In the middle of the circle is a large Easter basket filled with eggs (one per child). Read an Easter story that has one word repeated often. The first time you say that word everyone will take one egg from the basket. From then on, whenever you say that word, everyone will pass the egg to the left. At the end of the story the children will open the eggs they are holding and keep the treat inside.

Design a Comic Strip: Photocopy one cartoon, as illustrated above, for each child. The children will create their own comic strip by writing sayings for each character. Let the children color and decorate their strip. Allow the children time to share their comic strip with the other party guests.

Index

171